Discover Your True Image
in Christ

Discover *Your* **True Image in** *Christ*

by
Craig S. Hill

HUNTINGTON **HOUSE, INC.**

Shreveport • Lafayette
Louisiana

Huntington House, Inc.
1200 N Market St., Shreveport, LA 71107

Typography by Publications Technologies
Printed in the United States of America

All scripture quotations, not otherwise noted, appear in
The New American Standard Bible. The following versions
have also been used: *The New American Standard Bible*,
The Lockman Foundation, 1960, 1962, 1963, 1968, 1971,
1972, 1973, 1975; *King James Version*, Thomas Nelson, Inc.,
Publishers; *The Amplified Bible*, Zondervan Bible Publishers,
1965, 12th Printing, 1975.

*The characters in many of the examples cited in this book are real-
life people whom the author has known. For their privacy,
however, their names and some of the details have been altered.*

1   2   3   4   5   6   7   8   9   10

CONTENTS:

DEDICATION:

To my wife Jan, whose patience and kindness have made this book possible. I praise God for the treasure of her company!

SPECIAL THANKS TO:

Jean Orr: For pouring out her life and teaching and imparting to me many of the basic concepts expressed in this book.

Greg Carr, Kenneth Copeland, Marilyn Hickey, Dave Roberson, Randy Shankle, and Dr. Bruce Thompson, whose teaching contributed to my life and understanding.

Sherrye Koerting, Rosemarie Sandow, and Vera Thomas: For working their fingers to the bone typing and retyping the manuscript.

Janet Ficany: For editing

FOREWORD:

Craig Hill is a member and a blessing to Happy Church. He has been very faithful with his compassion and concern for people to see them set free with the Word of God. He is also a deacon over our missionary program.

I have watched him grow in the Lord and I love the beautiful spirit that he has displayed in the Body of Christ. His vision to reach the world with the Word is very outstanding.

When I read the manuscript for his book I was overwhelmed. I think it was because God so dealt with my own life in many sections of the book. It just seemed to put in an orderly manner little pieces here and there that I did not have quite together. I felt that the Holy Spirit ordered me to read this book at this particular time of my life. How many of us have really been deceived by the flesh and are still being deceived in areas? I saw such little subtle places where my flesh had overcome the leading of the Spirit in my life. I saw where I had failed the Body of Christ and have been blinded by carnality in my life.

I think this is an excellent book to set you free. I highly recommend it to every Christian and especially to Christian leaders. I think as leaders we are the most deceived of all by our flesh. Certainly we want our ministry to edify and when we are free then we know how to set others free.

This is a wonderful book to set you free, I recommend it highly.

— **Marilyn Hickey**

INTRODUCTION:

Craig Hill did not become a commercial jet pilot overnight! As a boy his interest was sparked by the laws of aerodynamics. He advanced from kites and model airplanes to hot air ballons, skydiving and gliders. As a teenager he obtained his single and multi-engine pilot's license, instrument ratings, plus Lear jet ratings. He had mastered the laws of wind, weather and gravity.

In the more than ten years that I have known Craig, I have watched him study, learn, practice, and finally teach the laws of the spirit (Ezra 7:10). Life is not just avoiding death! Craig will teach you to soar as he shares the principles of the "spirit" life. His real-life illustrations from the U.S. and his ministry behind the Iron Curtain add a great interest dimension to his presentation. I commend him to you as a friend, brother in Christ, and a teacher of the Word.

— **Loren Cunningham**

Chapter One:
Deceived?
Who Me?

Deceived? Me? No, it couldn't be!

Thinking I was walking in the spirit, while actually walking in the flesh. Thinking I was ministering the Word in God's power, while actually ministering in my own natural ability. Thinking I was trusting in God, while actually trusting in myself. Thinking I was walking in God's wisdom, while actually walking in man's wisdom, and perhaps even demonic wisdom. Thinking I was free, while walking in slavery.

Could these statements really have been true about me? Could I have been so deceived that I didn't know within my own soul the difference between darkness and light, bondage and freedom? After all, I'd been born again for 12 years. I was not a brand-new babe in Christ. I was a mature Christian: born again, filled with God's Spirit, a counselor of others, a teacher of the Word, invited to speak in seminars, and foreign countries. These things couldn't be true about me! Mistaking my own soulish manipulation of the hearers for the anointing power of the Word during my preaching? No! It just couldn't be!

As I pondered these thoughts in the evening stillness of my room in Poland, halfway around the world from my home, I just couldn't believe that I had been so deceived by my own flesh. I had considered myself more spiritual than most others, and not subject to such deception. I wondered, "Could it really be true?"

A small team of three counselors and teachers of God's Word, along with myself, had been invited to minister through several in-depth teaching seminars and a pastors' seminar in southern Poland. We had been ministering the Word several times a day and counseling in between for about a week and a half, when, one evening, I engaged in conversation with Jean Orr, one of the other members of our team. Jean was a woman of God who had been mightily used of the Lord in teaching and counseling the Word — and my close friend. As we talked that evening after the meeting, I asked Jean her godly counsel regarding my own marital state. I had felt somewhat frustrated in my marriage, because it seemed my wife, Jan, was too often withdrawn or depressed and, consequently, wasn't supportive of me or my ministry. She often conveyed to me that she didn't feel very valuable or important, or that I loved her very much.

I knew that Jan's feelings were, in fact, primarily caused by me and the way in which I related to her as her husband. But I didn't know how to help her feel loved and valuable to me. I really did love Jan very much and had done everything I knew to convince her of my love. I had become somewhat confused because no matter what I did, I couldn't seem to change her feelings.

Jean asked me if I wanted seriously to know from the Lord why I couldn't seem to change my marital situation. She mentioned God had given her insight into this problem, but she wanted to know if I was willing to allow the Lord to convict me and change me. I said I was.

Jean then began to share with me the insight God had given her. She said, "You seem to believe that most of the areas of your marriage that are not working or are unfruitful are all Jan's fault. You perceive Jan as having many problems that wreak havoc in your marriage. Because of those perceptions, you convey that message to others, and really do believe, yourself, that you are walking in the spirit, being obedient to God and coping with these problems of Jan's in a very spiritual and mature way. You believe that you are really very patient and righteous to put up with Jan when she is feeling unhappy and depressed. But you also manipulate others in order to get them to agree with you — 'Poor Craig has to cope with a wife who is so unhappy and has so many problems.' That is all true, isn't it?"

When Jean spoke these words, I had a terrible

sinking feeling in my stomach as the Holy Spirit convicted me that the things she spoke were true. I answered, "Yes."

Jean went on. "The truth of the matter is that *you* are walking in great pride and self-righteousness. You feel very righteous because you are so 'kind' to Jan in spite of her problems. Actually, you are not being kind to her at all. You're not being motivated to meet her need by the love of Jesus in your spirit. You are simply using the Word as a law in your mind to try to do what you believe is 'holy' and 'spiritual,' and the obvious result is death. You are not bringing life to Jan.

"Craig, you are very busy pursuing your goals and projects, many of which are from God, but you're carrying them out in the flesh. You constantly impose your goals and plans upon Jan, and if she can't fit into them, you just bulldoze right over the top of her and go on in your pursuit of achievement and accomplishment. In doing so, you are crushing your wife. You are constantly conveying to her that projects, goals and other people are more important to you than she is. You are creating and facilitating the worthlessness and lack of love that Jan has been experiencing. The problems that you have considered to be Jan's are simply the fruit of your fleshly motivations that compel you to achieve and accomplish in order to feel valuable, honored and esteemed. You are bulldozing over your wife, crushing her, and making her feel worthless. What's more, you are feeling very spiritual and righteous in doing so."

Jean continued, "In this area of your marriage, you're walking in the power of your own flesh and the reasoning power of your own mind, and you don't know it. You think you're walking in the spirit. This is not the only area of your life in which you are doing this. Craig, you are unwittingly doing this in your teaching of the Word, also.

"You know, Craig, your teaching is very good. It's well organized. It flows in sequence well. You have good illustrations for your points, and it's well thought through and clearly presented. Your teaching is scriptural and full of good Bible truths. But most of the time there's not one ounce of God's anointing on it. It's only intellectual. It's resident in your mind, and it flows forth from your natural mind and out your mouth, into the hearers' ears, and stops in their natural minds. It's not coming from your spirit, it's not reaching their spirits, and it's not anointed.

"Your teaching," she continued, "is only going from your mind to their minds. The hearers are receiving it intellectually and storing it away as very interesting biblical information — but their lives are not being changed by it. Their minds are not being renewed by the Word because it's not anointed. You are blocking the anointing with your natural reasoning power. You are speaking with cleverness of speech and enticing words of wisdom, but they are man's wisdom. That makes the cross of Christ void in your life and the lives of the hearers. You're not trusting in God for your teaching, but in your own natural ability to extract biblical principles from the Word and dispense them to others. You're very good at that, and people compliment you on it, but it's not changing their lives. It's your wisdom and it's not anointed."

Jean shared observations with me about certain times when I had inadvertently hurt other people through sarcastic, critical or cutting remarks or humor.

"Often, Craig, you subtly, in pride, attempt to exalt yourself above others by making light of their mistakes or lack of knowledge. Frequently, your jokes and humor are at the expense of some other person. You can sometimes be sarcastic and cutting. These things are not edifying others around you, but are hurting them."

Jean continued, sharing with me that all of these qualities were not proceeding forth from my born-again spirit, but they were emanating from sin in my flesh which, through deception, had captured my mind, will and emotion; and had, without my awareness, brought me into captivity to the law of sin and death.

As I returned to the quietness of my small room that

evening, I was emotionally devastated. Jean, being the gentle and loving woman of God that she was, had not spoken any of these words in judgment or condemnation, but only in love and encouragement. Nonetheless, a part of me was deeply hurt and didn't want to receive these words. I knew that aspects of what Jean had said were true. Yet, other parts, I believed, were not true, and this made me angry toward her.

After a time, as my emotions became a little calmer, I began to pray, and asked my Heavenly Father to reveal the truth to me. As I waited before the Lord, that inner conviction and still small voice came and said that all of Jean's words had been true, even the parts that I couldn't yet see and thought were wrong. The Holy Spirit told me that it was the truth. I asked, "All of it, Lord?"

He said, "All of it."

As I continued to allow the Holy Spirit to reveal truth to me, more and more conviction and godly sorrow fell upon me, leading me to repentance. The Lord told me that, as I allowed Him to continue to expose the control of my own flesh within me, the Truth would set me free. I hadn't previously even known that I was still in bondage. The Lord reminded me that this was the same situation experienced by the Jews who believed in Jesus, but weren't yet aware of their own bondage to sin in their flesh:

"Jesus therefore was saying to those Jews who had believed Him, If you abide in My word, then you are truly disciples of Mine; and you shall know the truth, and the truth shall make you free. They answered Him, 'We are Abraham's offspring, and have never yet been enslaved to anyone; how is it that You say, "You shall become free"?' Jesus answered them, 'Truly, truly, I say to you, everyone who commits sin is the slave of sin. And the slave does not remain in the house forever; the son does remain forever. If therefore the Son shall make you free, you shall be free indeed'" (John 8:31-36).

I began to ask the Lord, "How can I be free from walking in my own pride and self-righteousness? I want to live a holy and righteous life for You." I thought I was living in holiness, but now I see that I was far from it!

The Lord then revealed to me, "Craig, you have been *trying* to be holy. You have been walking in your own strength and power, trying to be holy and righteous. You will never be holy and righteous that way. But walk in My holiness. Live in My righteousness. Because My Spirit fills your human spirit, you already are holy in your spirit, because I (in you) am holy."

The Lord then quickened to me a familiar Scripture in a new way.

"But like the Holy One who called you be holy yourselves also in all your behavior; because it is written, 'You shall be holy, for I am holy'" (I Peter 1:15-16).

The Lord then showed me, "You shall be holy, and you already are holy in your human spirit, because My fullness fills your spirit. I reside in your spirit. Your spirit, because it is born again, recreated, is full of My nature, which is holiness and righteousness. Because I reside in your spirit, and I am holy, you, in your spirit, are also already holy. Stop walking in the flesh and trying to be holy. Walk in the spirit and you will be holy, because I, in your spirit, am holy."

What tremendous hope I received when God first gave me this revelation! I am still continuing to receive understanding of who God has recreated me to be spiritually, but just the first glimpse of this insight gave me new understanding of how to walk freely in the spirit.

That evening I repented of having walked in the flesh, trusting in myself and not in God, and of all the specific details which the Lord revealed to me through Jean. I asked God's forgiveness, and I asked Him to cleanse me and renew my mind.

I felt substantially freer. However, since then, God has continued to give me deeper and deeper revelation of how the flesh, through deception, captures control of the soul (mind, will, and emotions) and thwarts God's purposes for His people, without their knowledge.

Chapter 1 — Deceived? Who Me?

Many of us may deny it or be unaware of it, but the truth is that every born-again believer in the Lord Jesus Christ is deceived in certain areas of his life and is walking in the flesh, thinking he's walking in the spirit. The apostle Paul tells us in his letter to the Galatians that a battle takes place in the life of every born-again believer. The enemy has no real power or authority, so the only effective weapon he has is deception. Only through deception do Christians relinquish to their flesh their born-again spirit's rightful control and authority. No Christian can walk in the spirit and the flesh at the same time. The two are at war with one another, and control of the mind, will, and emotions is the prize.

"But I say, walk by the spirit and you will not carry out the desire of the flesh. For the flesh sets its desire against the spirit, and the spirit against the flesh; for these are in opposition to one another, so that you may not do the things that you please" *(Galatians 5:16-17).*

When we are born again, a battle ensues within us, between our spirits and our flesh. In the above verses, most Bibles have capitalized the word *spirit* to connote the Holy Spirit. However, from the original Greek it's not possible to determine whether this word is capitalized. I believe that it should not be capitalized, but that Paul spoke here of a battle between our human flesh and our human spirit. After we're born again, the Holy Spirit resides in our human spirit and operates through it. But here Paul has said that we can either obey our spirits or our flesh. Verse 17 states that these two are set at odds against one another, and our flesh is what prevents us from doing what our spirits would really like to do: motivate us to be holy.

As a matter of fact, Paul says in verse 16 that if we walk by (are "controlled, directed and guided" by) the spirit, it's not possible to carry out the desire of the flesh. In other words, we can't be directed by the spirit and the flesh at the same time. It's either one or the other motivating us at any given time, in any given area of our life. Therefore, if we want to walk in holiness, all we have to do is learn to walk in the spirit, and not in the flesh. Because by doing so, we *will not* carry out the desire of the flesh. Thus, only our flesh can, through deception, prevent us from walking in holiness and doing God's will.

One Sunday morning I awakened early to pray and read my Bible in preparation for a Sunday School class I was to teach. As I prayed, I purposed to walk in the spirit that day. I confessed it with my mouth. I believed it. I received it, and I left for the church with my wife and son, full of faith and charged up in God's Word. I ministered in the class and felt full of life afterwards from the ministering of the Word. Jan, my wife, had to check something at the nursery after class, and said, "I'll meet you downstairs in front of the nursery to find a seat for the main service."

After I finished, I went downstairs and looked all over for Jan, but couldn't find her. Suddenly, I felt mildly irritated. I decided to put my guitar away in the car and then come back. When I returned, she still wasn't waiting in the place upon which we had agreed. I thought to myself, "Where is she? It's getting late and we're not going to be able to get a decent seat in church. Why isn't she here?"

Finally, I found Jan in the church foyer looking for me. She had waited downstairs for me for sometime, but we had missed each other. By this time my emotions had captured my mind, and I was really angry. I wanted to snap at Jan and criticize her, because now we had to sit on the side of the church where the view was poor. I suddenly realized I was no longer walking in the spirit, and that my flesh was dominating my mind and causing me to think, speak, and act in death rather than life.

The Holy Spirit spoke to me then and said, "You're not in faith. You're being ruled by your flesh, and you're in sin. You need to repent."

I thought to myself, "How did this happen so quickly?"

The Holy Spirit also spoke, "You're believing a lie. You think that this whole thing is Jan's fault. If she would have been where she was supposed to be, when she was supposed to be there, you wouldn't have gotten in the flesh."

I had to admit, "Yes, Father, that's true. That is what I'm thinking."

Then God said, "That's a lie. The truth is that you were drawn away and out of the spirit all by yourself (James 1:14-15) and allowed your flesh to begin to dominate your life. Don't blame your wife. *You* repent." When I acknowledged the truth, repented and received the Lord's forgiveness, all the anger and death in my soul left, and I was free again to walk in the spirit.

Our flesh is what rises up, captures our mind, will, and emotions and causes us to do the things that we have purposed in the spirit not to do. Basically, Paul said, "Because of my flesh I do things I don't want to do — and I don't do what I want to do!" (Romans 7:15).

The Bible tells us that man is a three-part being, made in the image and likeness of God. Men have devised in their carnal minds many different models of who man is. Some say that he is *id, ego* and *super ego.* Some say that man is a particular arrangement of matter with a form of cosmic energy dwelling inside. Others consider man to be merely a very highly evolved animal. But God says that man is made in His image and is a spirit, having a soul, and dwelling in a body:

*"Now may the God of peace Himself sanctify you entirely; and may your **spirit** and **soul** and **body** be preserved complete, without blame at the coming of our Lord Jesus Christ" (I Thessalonians 5:23).*

We are three-part beings: spirit, soul, and body. Many times we perceive ourselves more as bodies with minds and emotions. Most of us identify more with our bodies, primarily, and our emotions, secondarily, than with any other part of our being. We identify generally with and believe we are who our bodies are, and who we experience ourselves to be through our emotions and mind. Our first identity is our body. We think, "I'm black." "I'm white." "I'm *Latino*." "I'm Chinese." "I'm pretty." "I'm ugly." "I only have one leg." "I'm fat."

Secondarily, we identify with our minds and emotions. "I'm smart." "I'm dumb." "I'm always treated unfairly." "I'm happy." "I'm sad."

The truth is that we are not bodies. We are not minds. We are spirits. We have a mind, and we live in a body. God wants us to begin to think of ourselves in the spirit, not in the body.

Our spirits are that part of us that is eternal and permeates our entire being. Genesis 2:7 records how the spirit was breathed into Adam by God and was full of the eternal life of God Himself. It was the very breath of God. When Adam sinned and rebelled against God, his spirit became corrupt and took on the nature of sin, having lost its original nature and eternal life of God.

Our spirits are the part of us that enables us to know God. We can only relate to God through our spirits. Jesus said that God is spirit; and those who worship Him must worship in spirit and truth (John 4:24). You cannot know God in your mind, emotions or body. Only your spirit can know God.

It is man's spirit that differentiates him from animals. I don't believe that animals have spirits. In our spirits is resident our moral nature and our conscience. The spirit tells us what is right and wrong before God, while animals lack such information.

Like our spirits, our souls are also an eternal part of our being. Both our souls and spirits will live eternally. Our souls consist basically of our mind, will, and emotions. As with the spirit, the soul was also breathed into man by God in Genesis 2:7. The Bible refers collectively to the soul and spirit as the "heart." Our souls have the amazing ability to monitor and receive information both from the natural world and the spiritual world. Before we were born again, our souls were accustomed primarily to receiving input only from the natural world through our five senses. This is what Jesus was referring to in Mark 8:18 when He asked the disciples, "Having eyes, do you not see? And having ears, do you not hear?" He was saying, "Do you only receive input from your natural eyes and ears? Do you receive nothing in the spirit?" Our soul can receive input both from our physical five senses and from our spirit. It can receive spiritual information and natural information.

Our body, of course, is the physical housing of the spirit and soul. The body is not eternal, but temporal and will pass away at death. When the Bible refers to our "flesh" it is usually speaking of the remnant nature of sin (the "old man") still resident in our body. Our flesh is corrupt and seeks continually only its own gratification.

Before we were born again, all three parts of us — our spirit, soul, and body — were in agreement, aligned with the nature of sin which had corrupted our entire being. The only motives we knew before we were born again were selfishness and self-gratification. Our spirit and flesh were aligned with our soul toward the aim of selfishness. It wasn't possible for us to act out of a pure motive of unconditional love, because our entire being was corrupted by sin. This is why God spoke through Isaiah that all our righteous deeds are like filthy rags before God (Isaiah 64:6). Before we were born again, no matter how good and righteous our deeds appeared, or how pure our motives looked on the outside, the Word says that our motives proceeded out of corruption and were, in fact, filthy before God. Thus, it was impossible to please God with our own righteousness.

When we are born again, a wonderful miracle takes place within us. The Word says that we pass from death into life, from darkness into light. John tells us that we are not born again "of blood, nor of the will of the flesh, nor of the will of man, but of God" (John 1:12-13). Paul tells us in 2 Corinthians 5:17, "Therefore if any man is in Christ, he is a new creature; the old things passed away; behold, new things have come." You ask, "What part of me is a new creature? What old things have passed away? What new things have come?" Romans 6:6-7 tells us that when we were born again, the body of sin was done away with that we might be freed from sin. What body of sin was done away with?

We know from experience that after the new birth, we still had the same corruptible body. Our *body* was not born again. We also know that we have the same mind, and emotions that we had before. Every person who has been born again has noticed that sinful thoughts did not disappear totally from his mind after the new birth. This has caused a great many new believers much worry and consternation and has even caused some to doubt their salvation.

However, neither body nor soul becomes a new creature when we're born again, but the spirit. Romans 6:6 speaks of the nature of sin resident in our spirit that was done away with at the new birth. Our spirit man is the new creation. We still have the same brain and body we had before. Romans 12:2 tells us the Holy Spirit will renew our minds to the truth of what God has done in our spirit, but the mind is not instantly born again.

Therefore, the "old thing" that has passed away is the nature of sin in our spirit. The new thing that has come to our spirit is the nature of Jesus Christ. The exciting news is that, in your spirit, YOU ARE NOW, all that Jesus Christ was and is. The problem has been that unless we allow the Word of God to separate soul and spirit, we are often confused by our thoughts and behavior. Hebrews 4:12 states: "For the Word of God is living and active and sharper than any two-edged sword, and piercing as far as the division of soul and spirit, of both joints and marrow, and able to judge the thoughts and intentions of the heart."

We know that our spirit is saved at the new birth, but our soul is still in the process of renewal. Many Christians not understanding this have believed that the spirit and soul are saved together at the new birth, or have not even understood the difference between soul and spirit at all. When, after the new birth, they find themselves in sin, they are very confused and are forced into the position of either doubting their salvation or denying their sin. Actually, someone who wins people to Christ is not a "soul winner" but a spirit winner. At the new birth, the soul only begins its process of being saved (James 2:21).

Praise the Lord! The Word divides accurately between soul and spirit!

"No one who abides in Him sins; no one who sins has seen Him or knows Him ... No one who is born of God practices sin, because His seed abides in him; and he cannot sin, because he is born of God" (I John 3:6,9).

These verses would be very condemning if we didn't know that they concern our spirit. They tell us that our recreated, born-again spirit contains the very nature of God in seedling form and thus cannot sin. Everything that proceeds forth from our renewed human spirit is pure, holy, righteous and of God's nature. This is why, throughout His Word, God has commanded, "Be ye holy, for I am holy."

We can be holy only because He is holy in us. "Holiness" generated from an unrenewed, corrupt spirit is as filthy rags before God.

But when our spirit is born again of God, our spirit is already holy as He is holy. All that proceeds forth from our born-again human spirit is holy, because our spirit cannot sin.

Therefore, Paul wrote, "knowing this, that our old self was crucified with Him, that our body of sin might be done away with, that we should no longer be slaves to sin; for he who has died is freed from sin" (Romans 6:6-7). This tells us that we now have a choice: to be slaves of sin, or be freed from sin. Before we were born again, we had no choice. We had to sin. Our spirit, soul and body were all three corrupted by sin. But after our spirit was born again we received the choice to allow our mind, will, and emotions to be dominated and controlled either by our spirit, from which proceeds holiness and the nature of God, or by our flesh, from which proceeds sin and the nature of Satan.

Do you realize what this means? This means that you can have total victory in your life by simply yielding your mind, will and emotions to your spirit. If you are an alcoholic, the alcoholism is only in your soul and body. It is not in your spirit, if you are born again. If you have trouble with sexual lust, know that it doesn't proceed from your spirit, but it comes from your flesh and captures your soul. All you need to do is yield to your spirit and you will be free from these sinful manifestations of your flesh.

"But I say, walk by the spirit, and you will not carry out the desire of the flesh" (Galatians 5:16).

We then see that after we're born again, our spirit always wants to do God's will and our flesh always wants to gratify itself by doing Satan's will. These two battle against each other for control of our soulish area. Our spirit may reign in certain areas of our life, while our flesh reigns in others. Paul tells us that we can choose, with our will (which is part of our soul) whether to follow the dictates of our flesh or the direction of our spirit.

"Therefore do not let sin reign in your mortal body that you should obey its lusts, and do not go on presenting the members of your body to sin as instruments of unrighteousness; but present yourselves to God as those alive from the dead, and your members as instruments of righteousness to God. For sin shall not be master over you, for you are not under law, but under grace" (Romans 6:12-14).

We see that sin doesn't have to reign in our life unless we choose to let it do so. Verse 14 says that we are not under law, but under grace, implying that there is a cause and effect relationship between grace and sin not being master. The opposite is also implied: when I am under the law, sin is the master over me.

Therefore, the law is a primary weapon that our flesh uses to gain ascendency in our soul. Romans 4:14 says walking under the law nullifies our faith and prevents us from receiving God's promises for us. When we walk under the law we sever ourselves from Christ and make the blood of Jesus of no effect in our lives.

"You have been severed from Christ, you who are seeking to be justified by law; you have fallen from grace" (Galatians 5:4).

Additionally, I Corinthians 15:56 tells us that the power of sin is in the law. The letter of the law never brings anything but death, but the Spirit gives life.

"Who also made us adequate as servants of a new covenant, not of the letter, but of the Spirit; for the letter kills, but the Spirit gives life" (2 Corinthians 3:6).

Why is the power of sin in the law, and how does the law work to bring death? Paul says the law, in and of itself, is good and holy. However, sin working through the law "deceived me and, through it, killed me" (Romans 7:11). Into what does sin deceive me? It deceives me into allowing my flesh to capture my soul and rule me.

The truth is Satan has no real power in my life, but can only work through deception. He can't touch my regenerated spirit. Satan's only method of gaining preeminance in my mind or emotions is to deceive me into choosing to allow my flesh to dominate my soul.

How, then, is the law used as a tool of deception to bring death to my soul? According to Romans 7:22-23, three different types of law are at work within me! "For I joyfully concur with the law of God in the inner man, but I see a different law in the members of my body, waging war against the law of my mind and making me a prisoner of the law of sin which is in my members."

We have first the law of God in which our inner man (spirit) rejoices. Second, we have the law of sin in our members (flesh). Third, we have the law of the mind against which the law in our members fights. The law of God is the holy nature of Jesus Christ that indwells our spirit. This is God's will, with which our spirit is already in agreement.

The law in our members is, of course, the corrupt nature of sin still resident in our flesh. These two constantly wage war against one another for control of our mind. But what is the law of the mind?

In verse 23 Paul says my flesh wages war against my mind and makes me captive to sin. If our flesh and mind are against each other, then we can use the law of the mind as a weapon against our flesh. However, Paul calls the mind an ineffective weapon, because the flesh is able to win and bring us into captivity to sin.

I believe that the law of the mind is any standard of thought or behavior that we should follow. We then implement such standards in our mind as a law to fight against sin. This standard may come from our families, friends, local churches, or even from God's Word! The standards can be right or wrong. But even godly standards, when used as a law of the mind, cause our flesh to win and we then fall captive to sin. Why? Because sin in our flesh is more powerful than the law used in our minds in an attempt to overcome sin.

For example, I shared how my friend, Jean, had lovingly, but honestly made me aware of some critical, sarcastic and cutting remarks that I had made. When the Holy Spirit convicted me that this was true, I said, "Thank you, Lord, for revealing the truth to me," and I decided to stop making caustic remarks. During the next few days I made a great effort to guard my mouth and watch every word. However, a few unkind comments slipped out anyway. I could see I was going to have to try much harder to stop. Over the next few days, I purposed to weigh every word before I spoke it. Even so, I still found sarcastic and unkind comments coming forth before I could stop them. I began to be discouraged and condemned. I began to think that perhaps I should not speak to anyone at all. I felt so ashamed before the Lord, because He had convicted me of the sin of these comments, but I couldn't seem to catch them until after they'd already left my mouth. I began to plead with the Lord to take these thoughts and words away from me. I didn't want them!

I thought to myself, "I'll just have to try harder and be more careful and speak less." It seemed that the more I tried to guard my mouth, the more ashamed I felt before the Lord because I still couldn't stop. I began crying out to the Lord in desperation, "Please deliver me from this sin." But He didn't seem to be helping me. I even became slightly annoyed with God and thought, "God, why don't *you* help me? Why does this same sin keep happening, and why can't I stop it?"

Finally the Holy Spirit spoke to me, "I have already delivered you from that, but you're not walking in My deliverance. Jesus' blood was shed for your deliverance but you are still allowing sin to be master over you."

I said, "But Lord, I'm trying my hardest to stop."

He urged me, "That's precisely why you're not having victory. You are trying to stop by using my Word as a law in your mind to guard your mouth. You're already delivered from this in your spirit, but you're not walking in the spirit."

With only a few words, the Lord revealed I had taken a standard of behavior that was truly of Him and made it law in my mind. Then I had tried to fulfill the law in obedience to God. Yet, I did so through the power of my own will and strength. I didn't lean on God's strength, so I was defeated by sin's work in my flesh.

The more I concentrated on the standard in my mind, the more conscious I became of my own inability to fulfill that standard, and the more conscious I became of how sinful I really was! Essentially, the more I tried to fight sin, the more I lost and became further discouraged — convinced of my inability to overcome. I could see only the power of sin in my life.

This is precisely how sin, working through the law of the mind, deceives people. During this struggle, the truth remained the same: Jesus in me was more powerful than my flesh. But I had believed unconsciously that my sin was "too strong for God to change," and I wondered how I could ever please Him. *I believed that I was not obeying God because I couldn't obey Him.*

All of these thoughts were deception caused by sin in my flesh fighting against the law in my mind. I waged war against sin but nevertheless, sin reigned and reaped a harvest of confusion in my mind and emotions. If such thoughts were the deception, what was the truth? It was that God still loved me unconditionally. Unless I lean on His unconditional love, I'll lose my battles and wonder why God doesn't help. A law in the mind, enforced by human strength and willpower, never overcomes fleshly sin. Only the law of the spirit can give us hope. Romans 7:23 says we never win battles against sin through laws in our mind. Instead, we become angry at God. For that reason, Paul boldly stated the power of sin *is in the law* (I Corinthians 15:56). At this point, God isn't angry or judgmental toward us. He loves us and is waiting for us to turn to Him, trust Him, and begin to walk in the spirit.

When I realized these truths, I repented of identifying with my flesh and trying to fight sin with a law in my mind. I asked the Lord's forgiveness and began to confess the truth of who I was in the spirit. I began to believe I truly had the nature of Jesus Christ by yielding my mind and mouth to my spirit. I didn't have to dwell on trying to guard every word. I didn't have to strive and struggle. My mind began to be renewed to the truth of who I am in the spirit, and I began to be conformed to the nature of Jesus Christ already within me. With my renewal, my words naturally reflected what was within.

*"Therefore putting aside all filthiness and all the remains of wickedness, in humility receive **the word implanted, which is able to save your souls**" (James 1:21).*

The implanted Word of God renews our minds. Our souls (mind, will, and emotions) are in the process of being saved through being renewed to the truth of God.

Using the Word as a law in our mind to fight sin in our flesh does not deliver us, but serves to deceive us into thinking our sin is deep-rooted and powerful. Many pastors and Christian counselors, not understanding this, often attempt to help people overcome their "problems" by showing them where they are being disobedient to God's Word and then prescribing biblical principles to help solve the problem. The counselee then takes these biblical principles (which he understands intellectually) and tries to apply them as a law in his mind. He becomes discouraged, saying, "I've tried everything. Nothing works — not even God or the Bible. There's no hope of deliverance for me." Such counseling only attempts to modify the flesh with biblical principles. God doesn't want us to modify our flesh or anyone else's. He wants us to mortify the flesh and walk in the spirit:

> *"For if you are living according to the flesh, you must die; but if by the Spirit you are putting to death the deeds of the body, you will live" (Romans 8:13).*

Don't be deceived into thinking that your flesh is not so bad. You can't afford to let your flesh dominate your life for one minute. Galatians 5:9 tells us, "... a little leaven leavens the whole lump." Your flesh will strive to capture and rule any area of your soul that you let it. Your flesh has the nature of Satan. It's the same nature that killed six million Jews in Hitler's Germany, the same that rapes, kills, maims, tortures, and destroys.

Satan wants to deceive you into believing sin in your flesh isn't so bad. Dear friend, sin is hideous — any sin. God hates it. He hated it in Hitler; He hates it in you and me. If we realize the true nature of sin in our flesh and the devil's purpose of destruction in our lives, we begin to hate it too. God wants us to hate sin so that we'll be diligent to repent of it and walk in the spirit.

As you hate sin, remember you're not sin. You're holiness in the spirit. So don't hate yourself or identify yourself with the sin. Hate the sin, so you won't fall captive to it, but love yourself according to the truth of who God has made you to be, already, in the spirit. If someone hurts you very deeply — perhaps they falsely accuse you and defame your character — anger and hatred will rise up in you toward that person. The Holy Spirit will immediately convict you that hatred is wrong, and you can then repent and try to love that person. You can call on God to take away the hatred and replace it with love. You can speak love. You can design loving actions toward this individual, and carry them out. But none of these things will remove the hatred from your heart. Why not? Because you are still identifying with who your emotions and intellect say that you are: a person full of hurt and hatred. That's not the truth of who you are! The truth is that you are a recreated spirit being with the nature of Jesus Christ, and Jesus is not full of hatred.

Crying out to God and asking Him to remove hatred and replace it with love is not trusting God. It is unbelief. Instead of believing God and yielding your soul to your spirit, you are believing what your intellect and emotions are saying about yourself. Will you somehow magically change if you cry out to God? If not, and this is likely the case, you end up feeling that God is unfaithful by not helping you to get free of the hatred.

Once a young woman told me, "I don't believe in God anymore. If He were really God, He wouldn't let me be defeated by sin." She had begged, and pleaded with God for help, but He hadn't delivered her. So, she concluded either she was so weak and wicked that God wouldn't help her, or there was no God.

To answer her, the Lord led me to ask if she had seen the *The Wizard of Oz*. I don't believe in the concepts put forth in that movie, but a useful analogy can be drawn. She had seen it, so I reminded her of how homesick Dorothy had worn ruby slippers that could have whisked her home. But only upon learning of their power could she use it and go home.

Likewise, God's Word says, "My people are destroyed for lack of knowledge" (Hosea 4:6). Many people in the Body of Christ are being destroyed and are dying because they don't know who they are in Christ or how to appropriate the power of the blood of Jesus, which has already purified and cleansed their spirits.

We need to know that using God's Word as a law in our minds will not deliver us from hatred, sexual lust, drinking, overeating, stealing, beating our family, strife, anger, pride, selfishness, or any other area of sin. We are already free from all these things. We simply need this freedom to become manifest in our souls.

Another revelation in Romans 7 is that, when a Christian sins, the recreated spirit is not defiled by that sin. Only the mind, will, emotions, and body are defiled:

> *"For we know that the Law is spiritual; but I am of flesh, sold into bondage to sin. For that which I am doing, I do not understand; for I am not practicing what I would like to do, but I am doing the very thing I hate. But if I do the very thing I do not wish to do, I agree with the Law, confessing that it is good. So now, no longer am I the one doing it, but sin which indwells me. For I know that nothing good dwells in me, that is, in my flesh; for the wishing is present in me, but the doing of good is not. For the good that I wish, I do not do; but I practice the very evil that I do not wish. But if I am doing the very thing I do not wish, I am no longer the one doing it, but sin which dwells in me; find then the principle that evil is present in me, the one who wishes to do good." (Romans 7:14-21).*

When Paul says, "I am no longer the one sinning," who is the "I" to whom he refers? It is Paul, the spirit man! It is *his* spirit. So, sin does not emanate from his spirit, but his flesh. He is acknowledging the truth of who he really is as a born-again man. He is not his flesh. He is not his soul. He is his spirit. That is his true nature. Any other nature is something foreign that has captured his soul illegally, illegitimately, and is not him.

The truth of who we are is in our spirit, not in our flesh, even when our soul is totally dominated by our flesh. The first step toward freedom is in recognizing this truth. Moreover, our spirit is not defiled by sin, even though our mind, will, emotions, and actions may be totally captured by sin. Many Christians feel that they have lost their salvation when they find themselves in sin. But Paul says, "No, even though my soul and body may be defiled by sin, 'I', the spirit man, am still pure and righteous and holy, because I am no longer the one doing it, but the sin which dwells in my flesh."

God wants you to know, dear brother or sister, that understanding sin will not deliver you. Striving to implement biblical principles will not deliver you from sin. *Nothing will deliver you except the blood of Jesus Christ* literally renewing your mind and causing your spirit to be in control. If this were not true, God would not have wasted the precious blood of Jesus. He would have simply sent a group of highly trained psychiatrists, teachers of the Word, or biblical coun-selors to teach us how to overcome. This would have been far less costly. But God knew that the only real victory over sin comes through the miraculous recreation of the human spirit by the blood of Jesus Christ and the renewing of the soul to the truth of who He has made us to be in the spirit.

Romans 10:9 tells us what we need to do to be recipients of what Jesus did for us.

If you have not yet prayed to receive Jesus in your heart, the following is a prayer you may pray to do so:

Dear God, I confess that I have sinned and I want to be born again through Your Son, Jesus. I am sorry for my sins and ask You to forgive me. I believe in my heart that Jesus died, was raised from the dead and now lives. Recreate my spirit now, Lord, by the power of Jesus' shed blood. Jesus, I confess that You are now my Lord. I believe I am a born-again child of God.

Thank you, God, for my salvation, in Jesus' name. Amen.

Accepting Jesus is the first step to freedom. When you do that, your human spirit is miraculously recreated. Discovering through God's Word how to live in the image of Jesus (transforming your human personality to match your recreated spirit) is the second step to the most satisfying life there is.

Chapter Two:
Reasoning In Your Mind
Vs. Perceiving In Your Spirit

Terry was an attractive, single *Christian woman* who came into my office hoping I could help her with a business matter. She had weighed all options, but remained undecided. She was hoping I would have a word from the Lord for her, or at least wise, godly counsel.

I became frightened for I didn't *know* which way she should go. She was expecting me to provide God's answer, and if I failed, she'd think me not very spiritual.

Then the Holy Spirit spoke to me and said, "Repent of that pride. Quit worrying about your reputation and trying to figure out what to tell her. Listen to Me in your spirit and I'll tell you how to counsel her." I repented and began to allow the Lord to speak to me in my spirit.

First, I asked her what the Lord had shown her about the situation. She said she had prayed a great deal, but God hadn't shown her anything. I asked if the Lord spoke to her regularly in other areas. She answered, "Not much, recently." I then asked if she knew why she wasn't hearing from God. She didn't know.

The Lord had shown me that she wasn't perceiving very much of anything in her spirit, but she had been reasoning everything, including her relationship with God, in her mind. I said, "Let's pray and ask the Lord why you haven't been hearing from Him."

As we prayed, the word "bitterness" kept popping into my mind out of my spirit. I asked Terry if she were bitter toward someone and holding resentment toward them. She couldn't think of anyone.

I said, "Let's pray again, and you open your spirit to hear from your Heavenly Father. He will show you any area of bitterness."

Shortly after we began to pray again, Terry began to weep. I asked her what had happened. She began to tell about a man to whom she'd been engaged a year and a half earlier. She had loved him very much and he had, she felt, wrongly terminated their relationship and deeply wounded her. God had shown her that she was still bitter and angry toward him for hurting her.

We then prayed again and Terry repented of bitterness and allowed the blood of Jesus to begin to cleanse and heal her. While we were praying, the Lord spoke into my spirit, "She feels that same way toward Me. She's angry and bitter at Me, too." I shared this with Terry and she began weeping again as the Lord convicted her. She then began to share that she hadn't realized it, but she *was* angry with God. She felt that if He really loved her or cared about her, He would have provided her a husband by now. She was lonely and desperately wanted a husband, but she had been rejected several times in the past by men. She hadn't realized it, but deep inside she was blaming God for all of the rejection and her lack of a husband.

In her mind, Terry had formed an image of herself very early in life as being constantly rejected by men. Almost every time she met a man who interested her, she expected that he too would ultimately reject her. This became a self-fulfilling prophecy. What had happened? She had interpreted experiences based wrongly on five-sense knowledge, and thus built a wrong self-image.

Deep inside, Terry viewed God the same way. She didn't believe He cared for her, since He "wasn't meeting her needs." Sadly, she concluded He would reject her, too. Proof was that He had not given her a husband.

The net result was that Terry wanted to trust God. But she couldn't because she was angry with Him and thought He didn't really care about her and was rejecting her. No one can trust someone with whom he is angry or who is hurting him. Terry was crying out to God for a husband, wisdom and guidance, but she wasn't trusting Him at all because she really believed that He had been unfaithful to her and had let her down.

It's important to see that all of these false conclusions were derived from the "logical" interpretation of experiences and words spoken previously. As I shared with Terry the truth of God's identity and love for her, she began to receive it. We prayed again, and she repented of the lies she had believed about God, men in general, and herself. She was completely delivered from bitterness toward God as she began to allow her spirit to reign in her mind. I told Terry that, because she had been bitter toward God, she couldn't and hadn't been trusting Him. In essence, unbelief had blocked her from perceiving in the spirit and hearing from God. I told her that if she now sought God and purposed to perceive in her spirit without reasoning in her mind, the Lord would speak clearly to her about her business decision.

Three days later, Terry called and shared that God had given her specific guidance and she was having a marvelous time communing with her Father.

When we allow our minds to use only logical reasoning to interpret words and circumstances, we will be led to foolish conclusions and will hinder our ability to perceive in the spirit and commune with the Lord. Terry had been deceived through interpreting words and experiences according to her own natural mind.

Our natural mind has the amazing ability to monitor and receive input simultaneously from the natural world and the spiritual world. Our mind and emotions receive natural information through our five senses (seeing, hearing, tasting, smelling and touching), while our soul receives input from our spirit. Thus, we have two different types of perception available to us when we're born again. We can draw conclusions based on knowledge perceived in the spirit or from our five senses.

From our infancy on, the world trains us to rely only upon five-sense knowledge and our natural minds. After we are born again, our Heavenly Father can speak to us through our spirits. However, our minds are so programmed to reject spiritual insight and base our opinions and actions only on "objective, rational" reasoning, we continue to think that way in Christian living.

In general, we have still perceived our personal identity based on images deeply ingrained in our souls, gained through five-sense knowledge and natural reasoning. In other words, I experience myself to be the person my mind and emotions have said that I am. I perceive myself this way based on my natural interpretation of my experiences and from others' words spoken to me.

God wants us to know that our five senses do not always give us correct information. Our natural mind's interpretations and conclusions drawn from five-sense knowledge are often wrong. This is particularly true in making determinations about our personal identities and our relationships to God and to others.

For example, suppose a four-year-old girl, who loves her daddy very much, sees him building something in his garage Saturday afternoon. Out of love for him, she draws near to him and tries to help him hold up a piece of wood he is nailing to another. But he, immersed in his work and not understanding her desire to help, speaks to her in a cross voice to "go back inside and play! Can't you see Daddy's working?"

At this point the little girl has had an experience through informational input from her five senses. She sees the look on her dad's face. She hears the words he's spoken to her and the tone of his voice. Her mind and emotions now engage to interpret this experience.

Based on the input of her eyes, ears, body, and emotions, she draws these conclusions: 1) Dad doesn't really love her; 2) If he *does*, his work still is much more important than she is; 3) She is really not a blessing to him but a bother; 4) She shouldn't try to help him in the future, because he doesn't want her help.

Images are formed in this little girl's soul. These images are not correct. They are not the truth, they are based on the wrong interpretations by the natural mind through five-sense knowledge. Nevertheless, they become deeply ingrained. It's likely that when this little girl grows up, she will continue to view herself similarly in her relationship with her husband and the Lord. She won't understand why she experiences God as not meeting her needs, or why she experiences herself as too unworthy to come boldly to Him. It will seem to her, also, that her husband is always very busy doing important things, but she is unimportant, doing only meaningless things. This all stems from false images developed as a child based on natural reasoning.

God does not want us to use natural reasoning or five-sense knowledge in determining our personal identity or our relationship with Him and others. God's Word says in I Corinthians 2:14, *"But a natural man does not accept the things of the Spirit of God; for they are foolishness to him, and he cannot understand them, because they are spiritually appraised."*

Our own natural reasoning and emotions will not lead us to the truth of who we are, who God is, or who others are and how we relate to them.

"For since in the wisdom of God the world through its wisdom did not come to know God. God was well-pleased through the foolishness of the message preached to save those who believe" (I Corinthians 1:21).

Our own human wisdom will not lead us to know God. We can know many things about God through human wisdom, but we can only know God through our born-again spirit. Jesus told us in John 4:23 that God is a spirit, and those who worship Him must do so in spirit and in truth. We can only relate to our Father through our spirits, and we must relate to Him based on the truth of who He is as a Spirit and who we are as a spirit.

I'm not saying that you don't need input from your five senses at all. In order to drive a car, you need information from your five senses. If you walk across the street, you need to look first and see whether the light is green. However, you also need to perceive other information in the spirit. An example might be a car coming from around a corner not obeying the traffic signals yet not perceptible to your five senses.

Why is five-sense knowledge so detrimental in the

areas of personal identity and relationships? Because it is primarily through our five senses that our flesh deceives us, capturing our soulish realm. Our minds are so programmed to draw conclusions based on five-sense knowledge that, usually, we consider the information provided by our spirit foolish, as Paul stated in I Corinthians 2:14.

Five-sense knowledge is, in one word, flesh. If your mind is dominated by your flesh, the Word says you are hating God:

> *"For the mind set on the flesh is death but the mind set on the spirit is life and peace, because the mind set on the flesh is hostile toward God; for it does not subject itself to the law of God, for it is not even able to do so; and those who are in the flesh cannot please God" (Romans 8:6-8).*

The Greek word translated "hostile" in verse seven means "deep-seated hatred." In other words, the mind set on the flesh acts from deep-seated hatred toward God. When your mind is dominated by flesh, whether you know it or not, God says that you are hating Him. For that reason, our personal righteousness is as filthy rags before God (Isaiah 64:6). In our spirits, however, we want to love God and determine to love Him.

Let's look at an example from the Bible. Mark's gospel records an event where Jesus was teaching a large crowd in a home. Because of the crowd, four men who brought a paralytic for healing were unable to get near Jesus. Undaunted, they climbed up on the roof and lowered the paralytic down before the Lord.

> *"And Jesus, seeing their faith, said to the paralytic, 'My son, your sins are forgiven.' But there were some of the scribes sitting there and **reasoning in their hearts**, 'Why does this man speak that way? He is blaspheming; who can forgive sins but God alone?' And immediately **Jesus, perceiving in His spirit** that they were reasoning that way within themselves, said to them, 'Why are you reasoning about these things in your hearts? Which is easier, to say to the paralytic, "Your sins are forgiven"; or to say, "Arise, and take up your pallet and walk"?'" (Mark 2:5-9).*

This passage makes clear the difference between the scribes' reasoning in their hearts and Jesus' perceiving in His spirit. The scribes perceived nothing in their spirits. Their spirits were dead to God. They only knew how to receive five-sense knowledge and evaluate it according to the logical reasoning power of their minds.

The Greek word translated "reasoning" in this passage is *dialogizomai*.[1,2] This is the Greek word from which we derive our English word "dialogue." This word is composed of two other Greek words: (1) *dia* [3] — a preposition denoting the channel of an act. It means "through or by instrumentality of" and (2) *logizomai* [4] — a verb meaning "to take inventory, conclude, reason, reckon, suppose, or figure out." It comes from the Greek root of our English word 'logic.' *Logizomai*, then, can best be translated as the verb "to logic," or to reason and figure out in the mind by logic. Thus, *dialogizomai* means the process of drawing a conclusion through or by the instrumentality of taking an inventory (ferreting out pros and cons) or reasoning, reckoning, and figuring out the "truth", in the mind, by logic.

This was how the scribes evaluated Jesus' identity, teaching, and words. Their evaluation led them to a false conclusion. Instead of finding the truth and being set free (John 8:32), they were drawn further into deception and into deeper bondage to sin in their flesh.

Jesus, on the other hand, did not *"logizomai"* about the scribes. He didn't think to Himself, "They're looking at me strangely. I wonder what they're thinking? They probably don't like what I'm saying. They must not like me. Oh well, it doesn't matter, anyway. I know I'm right and they're a bunch of hypocrites!" No! Jesus didn't reason out in His mind what anyone might be thinking or doing, or how they might be relating to Him. The Bible says that Jesus "perceived in His spirit that they were reasoning in their hearts."

The Greek word translated in Mark 2:8 for "perceived" is *epiginosko*.[5,6] This word also comes from two Greek roots: (1) *epi* [7] — a preposition meaning "the superimposition of," and (2) *ginosko*[8] — a verb meaning "to know, to be aware of, or to perceive." *Epiginosko,* then, means "to know or perceive." In other words, knowledge or awareness is superimposed on the mind, but doesn't come from logical reasoning. From where, then, is the knowledge or perception superimposed? Mark 2:8 tells us that Jesus "epiginosko" or perceived in His spirit. Jesus knew in His spirit what the scribes were thinking, because God showed Him. Jesus then drew correct conclusions about Himself, about the paralytic, about the scribes, and acted accordingly.

The scribes, on the other hand, drew wrong conclusions about themselves (pride, self-righteousness), Jesus (blasphemer), and the paralytic (sinful, sick man, made sick by his sin, and not worthy of forgiveness or healing). Here were men who wanted to serve God and thought they were doing so, but were deceived by their own flesh, and were, in reality, hating God.

Often, we Christians do the same things the scribes did. We employ natural reasoning to interpret five-sense knowledge and draw wrong and foolish conclusions about our personal identity, God's identity, other peoples' identity, and the true nature of our relationships to God and others. We end up hating God because our minds are dominated by flesh, and we don't even know it! We think that we are in the spirit and loving God, but — for some reason — things just don't work out.

The Scriptures offer many examples of people who honestly sought truth, but whose minds were so programmed that they could not perceive spiritual truth.

For example, in John 3, Nicodemus sought such from Jesus, but his mind kept leading him to foolish conclusions. Jesus told him he had to be born again. Nicodemus, however, perceived nothing in the spirit, and, reasoned in his mind just how a person could re-enter the womb and be born again. Jesus spoke of the spirit being like the wind, but Nicodemus couldn't understand that either. Why? Because the natural mind can't grasp things of the spirit. They must be spiritually discerned.

Like most Christians, you have probably discerned in your spirit and also reasoned in your mind. It's possible to perceive in the spirit one moment and then reason in the mind the next, on a different matter. This occurred in Matthew 16 with Jesus' disciples.

*"And the disciples came to the other side and had forgotten to take bread. And Jesus said to them, 'Watch out and beware of the leaven of the Pharisees and Sadducees.' And **they began to discuss among themselves,** saying 'It is because we took no bread.' But Jesus, aware of this, said, 'You men of little faith, why do you discuss among yourselves because you have no bread? Do you not yet understand or remember the five loaves of the five thousand, and how many large baskets you took up? Or the seven loaves of the four thousand, and how many baskets you took up? How is it that you do not understand that I did not speak to you concerning bread? But beware of the leaven of the Pharisees and Sadducees.' Then they understood that He did not say to beware of the leaven of bread, but of the teaching of the Pharisees and Sadducees" (Matthew 16:5-12).*

In this passage, Jesus referred to the teaching of the Pharisees and Sadducees. But his disciples, walking in the flesh, reasoned that Jesus must have been worried because they had forgotten to bring a lunch and would be hungry. This was the brilliant conclusion to which their flesh led them through logical reasoning. They had forgotten that the absence of bread was no problem for Jesus, who just a short time ago had multiplied seven loaves of bread and a few small fish to feed multitudes.

Having no bread was not a problem for Jesus. But the disciples could not understand spiritual truth because they were not receiving input from their spirits. They were instead allowing their flesh to dominate their minds and therefore received input only from their five senses (probably mainly from their stomachs).

In the next part of the chapter, however, you see Peter receive something from God's Spirit, in his spirit.

"Now when Jesus came into the district of Caesarea Philippi, He began asking His disciples, saying, 'Who do people say that the

*Son of Man is?' And they said, 'Some say John the Baptist; some, Elijah; and others, Jeremiah, or one of the prophets.' He said to them, 'But who do you say that I am?' And Simon Peter answered and said, 'Thou art the Christ, the Son of the living God.' And Jesus answered and said to him, 'Blessed are you, Simon Barjona, because **flesh and blood did not reveal this to you,** but My Father who is in heaven'" (Matthew 16:13-17).*

Jesus confirmed that Peter's revelation of Jesus' true identity came not from fleshly reasoning but from the Father in heaven. Immediately after this, you see Peter drift out of the spirit and back into the flesh:

*"From that time Jesus Christ began to show His disciples that He must go to Jerusalem and suffer many things from the elders and chief priests and scribes, and be killed, and be raised up on the third day. And Peter took Him aside and began to rebuke Him, saying, 'God forbid it, Lord! This shall never happen to You.' But He turned and said to Peter, 'Get behind Me, Satan! You are a stumbling block to Me; **for you are not setting your mind on God's interests, but man's'"** (Matthew 16:21-23).*

Jesus told Peter his mind had been dominated by his flesh and was drawing conclusions based on man's interests, not on God's. Jesus even noted Satan had been working through Peter's flesh to thwart God's purposes.

Therefore, Matthew 16 shows the disciples walking according to natural reasoning and also according to revelation. When they perceived in the spirit, they received wonderful revelation from God. When they reasoned in the flesh, they made ridiculous conclusions and were out of faith toward God.

Thus you can conclude that the world's thinking leads to foolish conclusions regarding things of God. Receiving God's Word only intellectually and reasoning it out will cause you to draw similar foolish conclusions.

The world constantly teaches us to mix logic with God's Word. The world believes that knowledge and understanding bring freedom. Further, the world sees people as having "personal problems," "emotional disorders," and "psychological imbalances." Worldly understanding says and believes if people can understand the root of these problems, and deal with them by changing thinking or behavior, the problems will be solved. Christian "flesh" isn't much different because it believes if people find biblical principles that have been broken, and then understand and apply the correct biblical principles, the problems will disappear.

When Christians do this, they only understand God's Word in their natural mind. This always results in failure and frustration. In essence, this amounts to an attempt to modify our flesh with biblical principles. God doesn't want us to use His Word to modify our flesh. He doesn't want to use His Word to solve "personal problems," "emotional disorders," or "psychological imbalances." He wants us to recognize that all these things are sin operating through the flesh.

God then wants us, by the power of the blood of Jesus already resident in our spirit, to crucify the flesh, *stop* living in it, identifying with it, giving it power through the law in our mind, and using His Word to try to modify it. In short, God wants us to live in the spirit.

When we stop *trying* to reason out God's Word and allow it to permeate our spirit so that we perceive the Word in the spirit instead of filtering it through our fleshly mind, the Word becomes spirit and life exploding inside us. When stimulated by the Word, the eternal life of our Christ wells up in our spirits, the Word floods our souls, and brings life, peace and freedom.

Jesus said that His words are spirit and life. But when His hearers only received His words in their natural minds, the same words were not spirit and life to those people. Likewise, when Jesus told his disciples, "If you will eat of My flesh and drink of My blood, you will have eternal life," they couldn't understand it in their natural minds. Instead, they grumbled and complained:

"These things He said in the synagogue, as He taught in Capernaum. Many, therefore, of His disciples, when they heard this, said, 'This is a difficult statement; who can listen to it?' But Jesus, conscious that His disciples grumbled at this, said to them,

*'Does this cause you to stumble? What then if you should behold the Son of man ascending where He was before? It is the Spirit who gives life; the flesh profits nothing; **the words that I have spoken to you are spirit and life**'" (John 6:59-63).*

If we gain only intellectual understanding of the Word, it will not be spirit and life to us. This is why seminaries often have difficulty producing leaders full of faith, spirit and life. If we use the world's method to understand the Word of God, we will get results commensurate with that method. Paul expresssed it this way:

*"For Christ did not send me to baptize, but to preach the gospel, not in cleverness of speech, **that the cross of Christ should not be made void**" (I Corinthians 1:17).*

"And when I came to you, brethren, I did not come with superiority of speech or of wisdom, proclaiming to you the testimony of God. For I determined to know nothing among you except Jesus Christ, and Him crucified" (I Corinthians 2:1-2).

No matter how cleverly our intellect can produce theories, systems and good teachings from the Word, if such teaching proceeds from our natural reasoning power, it will have been subtly born in our flesh. No matter how good or clever it sounds, that teaching will cause you and others hearing you, to trust in self while thinking that they are trusting in God. These thoughts then will nullify the cross of Christ.

These are exactly the thoughts that my friend, Jean, shared with me. The result? I understood that my teachings oftentimes were not anointed. When Jean ministered this truth to me in Poland, I was offended and hurt by her words. However, I knew enough to crucify my natural reasoning power in interpreting the information. Instead of trying to reason her words in my natural mind, I decided to ask my Father to give me revelation in the spirit about it. This was the beginning of my receiving some of the deepest revelation from God's Word and Spirit that I have ever received in my life. Praise the Lord!

Word or Whitewash

During this time of conviction in Poland, the Lord showed me that not only had my teaching not been anointed, but that if anyone responded to it, it was usually not because of conviction of sin motivated by the Holy Spirit. Rather they responded to what I now call "Word manipulation." God showed me that I had used His Word to manipulate people in order to change them. I was using the Word to try to convict people of sin so that they would repent. I also used the Word to manipulate unbelievers to confess Jesus.

The people who responded to that manipulation were not really being set free. They were allowing their flesh to be manipulated by my flesh, and there was no real conviction of the Spirit leading to true\repentance:

"But if you have bitter jealousy (envy) and contention (rivalry, selfish ambition) in your hearts, do not pride yourselves on it and thus be in defiance of and false to the Truth. This (superficial) wisdom is not such as comes down from above, but is earthly, unspiritual (animal), even devilish (demoniacal)" (James 3:14-15, Amplified).

Natural wisdom, emanating from our own flesh and coming into our mind, is not from God and defies the Truth. Not only is it unspiritual and earthly, but is demonic. Our own natural wisdom is not just neutral or not very good; our soul, when governed by our flesh, is the realm into which demonic spirits gain input.

God showed me, "If you continue to move in your own soulish ability and natural wisdom, your clever ideas and wisdom will not only be ineffective and foolish, but will be of demonic origin and will lead you subtly and deceptively into rebellion and defiance of the Truth."

Christians who use their natural minds to understand the Word will come up with mere doctrines and ideas of demonic origin. This doesn't just happen with the Mormons, Jehovah's Witnesses, or Christian

Scientists. It can happen in a born-again, Spirit-filled church; even in your church.

Have you ever heard doctrines such as the one that pronounces that God doesn't heal today? Or, the gifts of the Holy Spirit are not for today? Or, "If you don't speak in tongues, you are not born again?" These doctrines are taught by born-again people in born-again churches. Their origin is demonic. The conclusions were reached by Christian people who loved God, but were trying to understand the Word through their natural minds.

What about slight deviations from the truth to accomplish a good objective? What about a ministry embellishing, ever so slightly, a story in a newsletter to make it sound more powerful so that people would be motivated to give more? What is this? It is worldly manipulation. The end justifies the means.

"We get more money to spread the gospel and get people saved," we say. This is purely natural wisdom of a demonic origin. Yet, Christians do it all the time.

What about a ministry sending out an appeal letter as follows: On the envelope is written, "Urgent. Open Immediately," or "Emergency. Postmaster, deliver immediately." Inside, it says, "Emergency. We're $250,000 in the red. We must have the funds by (thus and such a date). If you don't give, we'll have to cut back some of our vital ministry program. We're depending on you. Please send the largest gift possible."

This is soulish manipulation for the purpose of generating money for ministry. It's not depending upon the Spirit of God to motivate people, in the spirit, to give. It is an attempt to motivate through guilt by appealing to the flesh. Often, such letters use phrases as, "We're counting on you," or "We're depending on you." If a ministry tells me that they're depending on me, I know immediately that they're in serious trouble.

What about appealing to people's pride to motivate them to give? What about offering to exalt the names of significant donors by listing them on a large plaque, or other techniques which encourage potential donors to walk in overt pride? This does not help a donor to live in the spirit or give in the spirit.

These are techniques designed by natural wisdom, and I believe stem from demonic origin. They are designed by the fleshly thinking of those in ministry to stimulate fleshly motivation within potential donors. This is not the wisdom that is from above. It is the same wisdom in which Saul walked in I Samuel 28. It is, in fact, rebellion against God.

When the Holy Spirit revealed all of this to me, I was deeply grieved in my spirit. Jesus said, "When you filter God's Word through your human tradition, doctrines, and natural mind, and then try to dispense it to others, you make the Word void." Man's wisdom strips the Word of its power. If you mix man's natural five-sense understanding of the Word with the Word, you make the Word invalid.

*"Thus **invalidating** the Word of God by your tradition which you have handed down; and you do many things such as that" (Mark 7:13).*

If we mix God's Word with man's ideas, we will strip the Word of power in our lives. Don't filter Scripture through human theories and doctrines. Don't use the Word to manipulate others to accomplish "God's purposes" in their lives. Receive the Word in the spirit and allow your mind to be renewed by it. Only then can it transform your life and the lives of others.

Much of what is called "Christian counseling" is actually Word manipulation. It uses God's Word in the natural mind, according to five-sense reasoning, to modify the thinking and behavior of a counselee. This is like putting Band-Aids on cancer or covering severe structural cracks in a wall with whitewash.

*"It is definitely because they have misled My people by saying, 'Peace!' when there is no peace. And when anyone builds a wall, behold, **they plaster it over with whitewash;** so tell those who plaster it over with whitewash, that it will fall. A flooding rain will come, and you, O hailstones, will fall; and a*

*violent wind will break out. 'Behold, when the wall has fallen, will
you not be asked, 'Where is the plaster with which you plastered
it?' Therefore, thus saith the Lord God, 'I will make a violent wind
break out in My wrath. There will also be in My anger a flooding
rain and hailstones to consume it in wrath" (Ezekiel 13:10-15).*

God does not want us to use our theories or His
Word to modify our flesh. He wants us to receive His
Word in our spirit, allow it to convict us of any areas of
fleshly preeminance, and repent.

Our Father longs to speak to us in our spirits. He
longs for us to stop relating to Him and evaluating Him
and ourselves on the basis of logical interpretation. The
more time we spend in prayer and in the Word daily, the
more the Holy Spirit can show us where we are living in
our natural mind. Then we find freedom because we can
repent and allow our minds to be renewed to the truth of
the spirit.

1. James Strong, "The Exhaustive Concordance of the Bible," Abingdon
   Press, New York, 1980, pp.829, p.22, Greek Dictionary.
2. W.E. Vine, "An Expository Dictionary of Biblical Words," Thomas
   Nelson Publishers, Nashville, 1984, p.924.
3. James Strong, op.cit. p.22.
4. ibid. p.45
5. James Strong, op.cit. p.784, p.31, Greek Dictionary
6. W.E. Vine, op.cit. pp.844,845.
7. James Strong, op.cit. p.30.
8. ibid. p.20.

Chapter Three:

Choose
Life

"For the law of the Spirit of life in Christ Jesus has set you free from the law of sin and of death" (Romans 8:2).

Two principal spiritual laws operate on the earth today: (1) the law of sin and death and (2) the law of the spirit of life in Christ Jesus. They operate simultaneously and at all times. We, as born-again believers, can operate in either of these laws at any given time, in any area of our lives. We can operate in the law of life in one area and the law of death in another, but we cannot operate in both in the same area of our lives at the same time.

With our will, we choose the law in which we will operate. The law of death works through our flesh; the law of life through our spirit. The one we allow to dominate our soul is the one which will govern our life.

The law of the spirit of life in Jesus is available for us to walk in all the time, just as areodynamic laws are always in force — allowing airplanes to fly. However, the law of sin and death still operates on earth and must be superseded by the law of the spirit of life in Jesus.

Similarly, gravity is at work at all times, but is overcome by the laws of aerodynamics only when a pilot chooses to operate within these laws. Should the pilot, for any reason, discontinue obeying those laws, gravity is no longer overcome and takes control. This is not because aerodynamic laws no longer work. It is because the pilot is no longer operating within those laws. *By default*, gravity begins to rule. Whether the pilot knows anything about aerodynamics or gravity is irrelevant — both laws work the same, either way.

The law of sin and death and the law of the spirit of life in Christ Jesus are very similar to the physical laws of gravity and aerodynamics. What people know or believe about these laws is irrelevant; the laws still work in the same way.

Many times we, as believers, allow ourselves to operate in the law of sin and death simply due to lack of knowledge or misunderstanding. Hosea 4:6, "My people are destroyed for lack of knowledge."

When Christians allow their flesh to reign in their soul, thus experiencing the consequences of the law of sin and death, those Christians often decide that God is either punishing them for disobedience or disciplining them in order to build His character in them. Sometimes Christians even decide that Satan is attacking them and he's bringing their problems upon them. Of course the truth is that neither God nor Satan has specifically done anything, but the law of sin and death is at work.

No pilot would think of turning off a plane's engines during a flight and expect the airplane to just continue cruising in level flight. He wouldn't do this because he would understand that the engines are necessary to create a positive aerodynamic force in order to overcome the force of gravity. If a pilot did not understand the interaction of these laws, none of us would have much interest in flying in his plane with him.

If a person willfully drives his car off the edge of a cliff due to lack of knowledge about gravity, the car will fall to the ground, and the driver will probably be physically injured. It would be ludicrous for the driver to then declare, while recuperating in the hospital, "God allowed me to be hurt in order to humble me and teach me to trust Him more."

It would be equally ridiculous for him to say, "Satan attacked me and caused me to be injured when I drove my car off the cliff."

No! This man is simply experiencing the natural consequences of his action according to the law of gravity, which God placed on the earth for our benefit. However, if we operate cars or airplanes without the knowledge of gravity, we'll get hurt.

In the same way, if we allow our flesh to rule certain areas of our lives, sin — working through our flesh

— will deceive us, and we will experience the natural consequences of the law of sin and death.

I know of a Christian businessman who has been very successful. However, recently he has overextended himself financially, had some deals go sour, and now is deeply in debt. To bail himself out, he has put together a new business deal and is attempting to raise money from various investors to carry it out. But, he isn't telling them all of the facts about the venture because he fears that if they knew some of the risks, they might not invest. He is in great fear of bankruptcy and is desperate to close this deal in order to save himself financially.

In this situation, he does not realize he is operating totally in the flesh. He is not trusting in God. Christ is not his source. Instead, he is trusting in himself and in his own ability. He is interpreting five-sense information according to his natural reasoning power and therefore coming to foolish conclusions. Fear is driving him to deceive others so that they will help him. His mind, will, and emotions are dominated by his flesh, not his spirit, but fear has gripped him too strongly for him to see it.

If he does fail financially and end up in bankruptcy, well-meaning Christians may try to comfort him by saying, "God has allowed this time of trial and testing in order to humble you." But while God will certainly use circumstances to convict us of sin, He will not arrange, orchestrate, or "allow" this businessman's financial collapse. The man simply is experiencing natural consequences of allowing the law of sin and death to operate in him through his flesh. God didn't allow anything. The man allowed his flesh to rule and is reaping the consequences. God is often blamed for the negative circumstances in our lives — when the blame should go to our having allowed flesh to have dominion.

The law of sin and death is not even something God designed to operate on earth. It was never a part of His plan, for He doesn't work that way. The law of sin and death was introduced by Satan, through Adam's sin.

Prior to Adam's rebellion against God, no law of

sin and death was operative on the earth. God had placed Adam and Eve on the earth and given them dominion and rulership over it. There was no sin, sickness, poverty, guilt, or mental and emotional torment. God never intended for man to experience these things; yet, I am certain God intended for Adam and Eve to grow in the Lord and in the knowledge of His creation. To do so, God didn't find it necessary to use injury, financial distress, sickness, and destruction to teach Adam and Eve His ways and allow them to grow. Why, then, do many Christians today believe that God is not able to teach His children without using these methods? Once again, God has told us in His Word that none of these things will be present among His children in heaven. Thus, God is not the author of sickness, poverty, oppression, failure, or mental and emotional torment. God wants us to grow through walking in the spirit — not through experiencing the consequences of the law of sin and death.

When God placed Adam in the garden, he intended Adam to know Him and learn, through his spirit, of His ways. God gave man dominion and rulership over the earth and expected him to rule the earth in the spirit, and in perfect communion with God. The law of the spirit of eternal life in God ruled on the earth at that time.

However, when Adam sinned and rebelled against God, he turned dominion and rulership of earth over to Satan, and Satan became the god and ruler of the world (John 12:31, 2 Corinthians 4:4). The entire earth and everything on it became corrupt and came under a curse when Adam sinned (Genesis 3:14-20, Romans 8:19-21).

When Adam handed his authority to rule the earth over to Satan, man was stripped of the eternal life that once dwelled in his spirit and soul, and the law of sin and death became predominant on the earth and in the lives of men. From that time forward, all men were born under the curse of the law of sin and death.

Many of the consequences of this curse are listed in Deuteronomy 28, verses 15 and following. These results of the law of sin and death working in a person's life can be summarized and paraphrased as follows: "You shall be cursed in the city, cursed in the country, cursed when you come home, cursed when you go outdoors; cursed shall be your baking, your food, your children, your crops and your livestock. You shall experience confusion, destruction, perishing, plagues, tuberculosis, fever, inflammation, infection, mildew and drought. You shall be defeated by your enemies. You shall experience boils, tumors, cancer, scabs, eczema, insanity, blindness, bewilderment, oppression, robbery, adultery, loss of possessions, financial distress, slavery, sores, poor harvests, crop failures, crop destruction by pests, humiliation. You shall be the tail, and not the head (controlled by your circumstances). You shall experience hunger, thirst, lack of clothing, lack of all things, enmity in your family, strife, chronic illness, depression, lack of peace and rest, homelessness, fear, despair of soul, mental torment, emotional distress, frustration and hopelessness."

These results of the curse of sin and death from Deuteronomy 28 can be summed up as: (1) Defeat (spiritual, soulical, and physical); (2) Sickness and disease; (3) Poverty and financial distress; and (4) Mental and emotional torment and distress. God did not intend for our life on earth to include any of these things.

It is Satan, now the ruler of this world, who implemented the law of sin and death on the earth through Adam's sin and, since that time, governs men on the earth according to that prevailing law of men's corrupted flesh. There is a thief who seeks to steal, kill and destroy in your life, but that thief is not Jesus. It is Satan.

"The thief comes only to steal, and kill, and destroy; I came that they might have life and might have it abundantly" (John 10:10).

In Deuteronomy 30, God told the children of Israel that, through the covenant which He had made with them by Moses, He had provided a way by which they could choose to receive His life and prosperity and overcome the law of sin and death:

*"See I have set before you today **life and prosperity, and death and adversity;** in that I command you today to love the Lord your God, to walk in His ways and to keep His command-ments and His statutes and His judgments, that you may live and multiply, and that the Lord your God may bless you in the land where you are entering to possess it. But if your heart turns away and you will not obey, but are drawn away and worship other gods and serve them, I declare to you today that you shall surely perish. You shall not prolong your days in the land where you are crossing the Jordan to enter and possess it. I call heaven and earth to witness against you today, that **I have set before you life and death, the blessing and the curse. So choose life** in or-der that you may live, you and your descendants, by loving the Lord your God, by obeying His voice, and by holding fast to Him; for this is your life and length of your days, that you may live in the land which the Lord swore to your fathers, to Abraham, Isaac and Jacob, to give them" (Deuteronomy 30:15-20).*

Under the new covenant that God has established with us, a much greater thing has happened. Jesus has come to give us abundant life (John 10:10). Abundant life does not include any of the results of the curse of the law of sin and death. It is not our Heavenly Father's desire for any born-again Christian to experience the results of the law of sin and death in our lives.

Christ redeemed us from the curse of the law, having become a curse for us — for it is written: "Cursed is every one who hangs on a tree" in order that in Christ Jesus the blessing of Abraham might come to the Gentiles, so that we might receive the promise of the Spirit through faith (Galatians 3:13-14).

Paul tells us in Romans 8:3 that, in Jesus Christ, God condemned sin in the flesh. If so, what causes us to continue experiencing the consequences of the law of sin and death after we're born again? Romans 7:11 tells us that it's *sin* in our flesh *deceiving our mind,* thereby capturing it and bringing death to our soul. If God condemned sin in the flesh through Jesus, then we don't have to accept in our lives what God has condemned. When Jesus' blood was shed, you were redeemed from the curse of the law of sin and death, and Jesus established a new law — the law of the spirit of life in Christ Jesus. So, after we were born again, we could choose to allow our flesh to reign and experience the law of sin and death, or we could let our spirits reign and be set free from the law of sin and death by the law of the spirit of life in Christ Jesus. We can choose life or death.

God, of course, wants us to walk in the law of the spirit of life in Jesus. It is not His desire for us to walk in the flesh and experience the law of sin and death. It is not God who leads us into that terrible law, nor does He "allow" us to experience its consequences to "teach us" to come into the law of the spirit of life in Christ Jesus.

God, however, will use every negative circumstance and result of the law of sin and death working in your life to glorify Himself and minister His love, grace and wisdom to you (Romans 8:28).

Let me give an example. Suppose the Christian businessman, to whom I was earlier referring, decides to promote his venture primarily among Christians. If these prospective investors seek the Lord, God may rightly lead all of them not to invest in this venture.

This will eventually lead to the financial collapse of the Christian businessman. You may then ask, "Did God author a circumstance that resulted in financial distress for one of His children?" In this case, yes, He did. However, this was not by God's design, but rather was because the man, himself, created a harmful circumstance involving other people, which God could not bless. The ensuing consequences were thus not according to God's purpose for the man, but were unavoidable because of the others involved. Let's look at one more example. Suppose a Christian employee is walking in the flesh in his job, and is consequently destroying many relationships and creating much animosity and disharmony at work. His Christian employer may be led of God to fire him for the sake of harmony in the business. This may result in financial and other distress for the employee.

It was God who led the employer to take this action.

However, it is the employee's own flesh that created the circumstance which ultimately resulted in his experiencing the consequences of the law of sin and death.

It is never God's desire or purpose for us to experience consequences of the law of sin and death. Although this is sometimes unavoidable, as in the above examples, we can always run to God for wisdom and know that it is His purpose and desire to deliver us and give us victory. We need never think that the Lord wants us to remain in the circumstances and simply endure them.

Thus, when torment comes upon us, we should not say, "God sent it," or that it was according to His divine purpose. Instead, we must recognize these are the natural consequences of the law of sin and death operating in our lives. Consequently, we must ask God *how* these consequences have been operating through us:

"Let no one say when he is tempted, 'I am being tempted by God'; for God cannot be tempted by evil, and He Himself does not tempt any one. But each one is tempted when he is carried away and enticed by his own lust. Then when lust has conceived, it gives birth to sin; and when sin is accomplished, it brings forth death. **Do not be deceived,** *my beloved brethen" (James 1:13-16).*

It is important for us to recognize a clear distinction between the results of the law of life and the law of death. They can be summarized in the following chart:

Law of Sin And Death	Law of Spirit of Life in Christ Jesus
Sin	Salvation and redemption
Sickness and disease	Eternal life
Poverty	In-filling of the Holy Spirit
Financial distress	Gifts of the Holy Spirit
and lack	Fruits of the Holy Spirit
Death	Financial needs met
Mental illness	Mental and emotional peace and rest

If you do not draw a distinct line between the results of these two laws, you will be deceived into believing that your experience of the law of sin and death in your life is God's will for you. Many Christians are confused because they don't see a direct correlation between their circumstances and their lives. They do not understand the law of sowing and reaping. There is usually a time delay between the time a bad seed is sown and the time a crop is harvested. Oftentimes, after a seed is sown, we continue to reap a harvest for a long time to come, even though we've sown no more bad seeds. If you sow to the flesh for several years in a certain area of your life, and then stop your fleshly sowing in that area, you may continue to reap a harvest for some time to come. If you sow to your flesh today, you, likewise, may not reap that harvest for some time yet to come.

This is what Christians have great difficulty understanding. Oftentimes, we expect to reap today whatever we've been sowing yesterday and today, or to reap this week whatever we had sown last week. Sometimes seeds don't grow that fast. It's a certainty though that you will reap what you sow:

> *Do not be deceived, God is not mocked; for whatever a man sows, this he will also reap. For the one who sows to his own flesh shall from the flesh reap corruption, but the one who sows to the Spirit shall from the Spirit reap eternal life (Galatians 6:7-8).*

If a man sows to his flesh in the financial area for 15 years of his adult life, and then realizes that he's had a wrong attitude and repents, he may become frustrated after one month and wonder why his financial situation has not improved at all since he began sowing to the spirit. The answer, of course, is that the seed he has been planting for one month simply hasn't had time to mature and bear fruit. This is not the time to give up and say, "The Word doesn't work!" Rather it is the time to press on in the spirit and pursue the harvest.

Another area of misunderstanding regarding the

consequences of the law of sin and death relates to the nature of deception. Romans 7:11 tells us that sin in our flesh deceives us and, thereby, brings death. Many times when our flesh is in control of a certain area of life, we are deceived and don't know it. This is very tricky. Deception, by definition, means, "you don't know about, or are unaware of the deception." If you knew you were deceived, you wouldn't be deceived any longer. However, sometimes we think that it is unfair to reap the consequences of the law of sin and death when we didn't know that we were sowing in the flesh in the first place!

Many Christians think, "This situation I'm experiencing right now can't be the consequences of the law of sin and death, because I've been diligently seeking God and being obedient to everything He has shown me. Sin couldn't be operating through my flesh, because I am not willfully operating in the flesh in any area."

Wrong! This very attitude expresses the natural, carnal reasoning *(dialogizomai)* of the mind: the interpretation of five-sense knowledge according to worldly thinking and not according to perception *(epiginosko)* in the spirit. Sin has deceived this person in certain areas, and through it, is bringing death to his soul in those areas.

In the first chapter, I shared about how the Lord had convicted me of ministering in the flesh according to my own carnal reasoning. I had no idea of it until the Holy Spirit revealed it to me. When Jean first talked with me about my ministry, I didn't want to believe her words. My natural mind told me "she must be wrong." But when I quit reasoning in my natural mind and opened up in my spirit to hear what the Holy Spirit had to say, He confirmed the truth that she was right. I had been deceived without knowing it. The flesh will, and does, deceive believers. When you are deceived in a certain area, you don't know it because you are deceived. Perhaps you have seen fleshly behavior in a close Christian relative of yours, such as a husband or wife. Chances are that this person has been totally unaware that their behavior has been motivated and controlled by their flesh. They probably thought that they had been in the spirit. Even if you point it out to them now, if they don't perceive the truth from God in their spirit, they will still think that they were in the spirit. This is because, in that area, sin in their flesh has deceived them.

Most Christians don't willfully and purposefully walk in the flesh. Your husband or wife probably doesn't get up in the morning and say, "I think I'll just walk in the flesh today in my relationship with my wife (husband)." When I was teaching overseas, I didn't make a conscious choice to minister in the flesh. No, I was deceived. I did not realize what was happening.

Like me, every born-again believer has areas in his soul where sin in the flesh has deceived him and he doesn't know that his flesh is preeminent in that area. This is true of every single person until he dies or is raptured. No one is exempt. Even your favorite spiritual hero, whoever that may be, has areas in his life where his flesh is preeminent and he is deceived and doesn't know it. Thus, he will reap, or is reaping, the consequences of the law of sin and death.

Therefore, when you are reaping the natural consequences of the law of sin and death in some area of your life, don't use your natural mind to try to reason out, "In what area am I in the flesh?" Don't conclude that you haven't been in the flesh simply because you can't figure out where you're missing it. If you do, you will then conclude that God either sent you this problem, or allowed it to occur in order to break you so that you would submit to Him. No! Remember, God works exclusively through the law of the spirit of life in Christ Jesus. Satan works exclusively through the law of sin and death. God and Satan are not in league with one another regarding you. God is not the thief — Satan is.

When you experience the consequences of the law of sin and death in some area of your life, and you don't know why, that should immediately signal you that your flesh is ruling in an area of your soul, and you're deceived without knowing it. Don't blame God or other people. Don't even blame Satan. Sure, Satan can and will attack you. But any power he has over you can only come through the law of sin and death in your flesh. If you have purposed to live in the spirit and not let your flesh reign in any area of life, then the devil can only work through deception and areas of fleshly domination of which you are unaware.

When you experience the consequences of the law of sin and death in some area, the thing you should do is go immediately to God and ask the Holy Spirit to reveal the deception to you in your spirit, and convict you of sin (James 1:5). Then, when God gives you revelation of sin, you can repent and allow the blood of Jesus to cleanse you and begin to renew your mind. If you have prayed diligently and still haven't perceived anything in the spirit, it would probably be valuable for you to see a Christian counselor who counsels by the Word in the spirit. The Holy Spirit can use such a counselor to help you receive revelation from God as to why you have not been hearing from Him in the spirit, and in what area you've been walking in the flesh and haven't known it.

Don't be afraid of opening up to the Lord and asking Him for revelation of sin operating through your flesh. God speaks a lot in His Word about judgment and condemnation of "the wicked." This sometimes causes born-again believers to be afraid of God and not run to Him for revelation of sin. But your loving Father wants you to know that. If you are born again, then you are "in Christ Jesus" and those "in Christ Jesus" are not "the wicked." They are "the redeemed." God has no judgment or condemnation for those "in Christ Jesus."

"There is therefore now no condemnation for those who are in Christ Jesus" (Romans 8:1).

Remember Romans 7 says that, when you find sin operating in you, it is not you that does the sinning, but sin dwelling in your flesh (Romans 7:17,20). God hates the sin in you and so should you, but *God loves you.* It doesn't matter what terrible and wicked sin may have risen up and captured your mind, will, and emotions since you are born again. Know this: you are not wicked. The sin in you may be, but you are not. However, don't use this as an excuse to stay in the sin when you see it, or it will destroy you, your relationship with the Lord, and others close to you.

When you read the Word, if you are born again, God does not want you to consider yourself as "the wicked," but as "the righteous" and "the redeemed," because that is the truth of who you are in the spirit.

"But by His doing you are in Christ Jesus, who became to us wisdom from God, and righteousness and sanctification, and redemption" (I Corinthians 1:30).

You have seen, so far, that at any time or area of your life you can walk in either the law of the spirit of life in Christ Jesus or in the law of sin and death.

What operates these laws? How do we choose to operate in the law of life instead of the law of death? Romans 3:25 tells us that Jesus Christ has become a propitiation for us through *our faith in His blood.*

Whom God hath set forth to be a propitiation through faith in his Blood, to declare his righteousness for the remission of sins that are past, through the forbearance of God" (Romans 3:25, King James Version).

I believe the law of the spirit of life in Jesus is activated by and operates through our faith in His blood.

On the other hand, the law of sin and death operates through lack of faith in the blood of Jesus, or unbelief. Unbelief is fear. Fear is distrust or lack of trust. If you have faith in someone's desire, wisdom and ability to treat you according to your best interests, then you are not afraid of them. On the other hand, if you distrust someone, or have faith that, in fact, they do not have your best interests in mind, then you will fear them. Thus, fear is, in fact, negative faith. The law of life operates through faith toward God, and the law of death operates through fear toward God.

We know that the law of sin and death (the law of death) is preeminent on the earth unless superceded by the law of the spirit of life in Jesus (the law of life). If you simply live your life without making a choice to operate in the law of life, you will, by default, operate in the law of death. There is no middle ground. The law of death is like gravity, and the law of life like aerodynamics. If you do nothing, gravity prevails. You can know all about airplanes. You can have many hours of flying experience, even be a flight instructor or professor of aerodynamics. You can go sit in a plane and talk about flying. But until you turn the engine on, advance the throttle and begin to use the laws of aerodynamics, gravity will prevail. Operating the laws of aerodynamics is the only way you will be set free from the law of gravity.

The Bible says that Christ has been made a propitiation for you through your faith in His blood (Romans 3:25). This says the law of the spirit of life in Jesus has set you free from the law of death. This is like saying that the law of aerodynamics has set you free from the law of gravity. The blood of Jesus is here and available. But Jesus is not a propitiation for you if you don't have faith in His blood. The law of life does not free you from the law of death — unless you walk in life.

Technically, you already chose life when you were born again. Your spirit is full of life, but your soul must now appropriate that life through your faith, or trust, in God. Faith toward God operates the law of life. Fear toward God keeps you from operating the law of life. If you don't trust the Lord in some area of your life or, because of past experience in your life, you believe that God was unfaithful toward you and didn't meet your needs, you won't have faith toward God in that area. Why? Because you will be afraid that He won't meet your needs and you'll be hurt.

If, for some reason, you were convinced that you would crash if you flew in a plane, it would be very difficult for you to have faith in the laws of aerodynamics. You would probably not subject yourself to such laws, and gravity would prevail. Likewise, unbelief rooted in fear toward God operates the law of death. If no choice is made, the law prevails by default.

Let's take this a step further. What operates faith and fear?

"For (if we are) in Christ Jesus, neither circumcision nor uncircumcision counts for anything, but only faith activated and energized and expressed and working through love" (Galatians 5:6, Amplified Version).

Faith is operated by love. Our receipt of the unconditional love of the Lord toward us enables and motivates us to trust God in that area and exercise faith toward Him. In any area where we haven't fully received God's love, and aren't convinced of His faithfulness toward us, we cannot be in faith toward Him. We will be in fear, not so much in fear of His punishment as in fear of His unfaithfulness to meet our needs.

In the last chapter I shared about Terry, who was having difficulty hearing from the Lord because of bitterness toward God. Terry was not operating in the law of life regarding the business of husbands. She was not trusting God for a husband, although she thought that she was. Because of past experience, she wasn't trusting God's love for her and trusting that He wanted to meet her needs. Instead, she was afraid that He didn't want to meet her needs because she thought that He hadn't done so in the past. This was not true about the Lord, but because Terry believed that about God, she was in fear toward Him and couldn't come into faith. Therefore, she couldn't operate in the law of life.

Fear, of course, operates through the opposite or lack of love. Lack of love is really hatred. We don't like to think of it that way because that implies thatwe are hating God and thinking that He hates us. But Romans 8:7 tells us our flesh is hostile toward God. The Greek word translated 'hostile' means 'deep-seated hatred.' So, when we're in the flesh, we are actually hating God because we're not receiving His love in that area.

If we believe deep in our hearts that God wants to punish us, or that He is unfaithful toward us in some area of our lives, then we will not trust Him in those areas. Our mistrust in God's love will keep us in fear.

I John 4:18 says that fear is tormenting because it creates turmoil and a lack of inner peace. However, this verse also reveals to us what brings us out of fear:

"There is no fear in love; but perfect love casteth out fear: because fear hath torment. He that feareth is not made perfect in love" (I John 4:18 King James Version).

The receipt of God's unconditional love will bring you out of fear and into faith in Him, into the law of life. The reason most people walk in fear is because their souls have, over the years, been deeply conformed to the world, and the world is devoid of God's love:

"Do not love the world, nor the things in the world. If any one loves the world, the love of the Father is not in him. For all that is in the world, the lust of the flesh and lust of the eyes and the boastful pride of life, is not from the Father, but is from the world" (I John 2:15-16).

Unfortunately, because of the deceitfulness of sin in the flesh, there are areas of our lives in which we love the world and aren't abiding in the love of God, but don't know it. As a result, we think that we are in faith toward God, but really are not.

The motivating forces operating the two laws can be summarized as follows:

Law of Sin And Death	Law of Spirit of Life in Christ Jesus
Death and turmoil	Life and peace
Distrust and fear	Trust and faith toward God
Lack of God's love	Receipt of God's love

What does all this mean? It means that you can be in faith toward God in one area, and fear in another. But you cannot be in faith and fear in the same area at the same time. Either you totally trust God or you don't. A little trust or trust with some reservation is, in fact, mistrust. Faith depends on revelation in the spirit of God's unconditional love for you. When you are sure of His love, your faith will be sure.

Many times, the consequences of the law of sin and death in our lives cause us to be like a pilot who desperately needs to be set free from the law of gravity. He may go to the airport and counsel with other pilots about flying. Then, he may go and sit in a plane and cry out for God to free from gravity, begging, "Set me free and let me fly." But he is still in bondage to gravity.

He decides fasting will help him fly. So he fasts, yet remains earthbound in bondage to gravity.

Finally, he decides a spiritual battle is going on —that Satan is blocking the flight. So he rebukes the devil and all demons and exercises his authority in Christ over them ... but he still doesn't fly. In exasperation, the pilot is about to give up. He reads Mark 11:23-24, and he sees that he should believe and receive in advance that for which he's prayed. So, he climbs back in the plane and declares, "In the name of Jesus, I receive freedom from gravity. I am flying. I confess it. It's mine. The Word says I can fly, and I'm exercising my faith right now to fly." But he remains on the ground.

None of these things have caused the laws of aerodynamics to overcome the law of gravity. So, this pilot finally quits reasoning in his natural mind and goes to the Lord, asking, "Father show me in the spirit why I haven't been delivered from gravity and why I haven't been able to fly." Then he hears a still, small voice in his spirit say, "Turn on the engine; taxi to the end of the runway and push the throttle forward." If the pilot does this, he will be operating in a physical law that God placed on earth for man's benefit.

You may argue, "Yes, but God is sovereign. He could make the airplane fly supernaturally." That's true. God could make it fly without ever turning on the engine. He has power to do so. He could do so. Perhaps He has done so in the past and will again in the future. But that is not the normal way for God to work relative to flying. God has made provisions for flying through the laws of aerodynamics, which are already in place and consistently work every time when we operate in them.

Similarly, God has implemented the law of the spirit of life in Christ on the earth through Jesus' blood, to deliver us from the law of sin and death. But, if we cry out to God for deliverance from bondage, rebuke Satan, get others to pray for us, fast, confess the Word, or whatever, none of these things in and of themselves operate the law of life. Romans 3:25 declares that faith in the blood of Jesus is what operates the law of life. In other words, we need to find out what God's Word says that the blood of Jesus has *already* done (past tense) for us.

Let's look at an example from the Word:

> *"And because of the surpassing greatness of the revelations, for this reason, to keep me from exalting myself, there was given to me a thorn in the flesh, a messenger of Satan to buffet me — to keep me from exalting myself! Concerning this I entreated the Lord three times that it might depart from me. And He has said to me 'My grace is sufficient for you, for power is perfected in weakness.' Most gladly, therefore, I will rather boast about my weaknesses, that the power of Christ may dwell in me (2 Corinthians 12:7-10).*

Paul was afflicted by a messenger of Satan and was experiencing the consequences of the law of sin and death in some particular area of his life. We know that God did not send or even allow this affliction, because God doesn't work through the law of sin and death. He did not allow Satan's messenger to come upon Paul to build his character. That messenger was meant for Paul's destruction, but God is not the destroyer; Satan is. Paul, himself, allowed Satan's messenger to afflict him through operating in the flesh. Satan can only afflict us when we allow flesh to reign in some area of our soul, either willfully or through deception.

In verse seven, Paul explained through which area of his flesh the satanic messenger gained control — pride. Paul had received tremendous revelation from God. In his own mind, his flesh sought to exalt him above others. Exaltation of self is pride. Pride emanates from the flesh, not from the born-again spirit.

Verse eight tells us, however, that Paul begged the Lord three times, "deliver me." Notice that begging the Lord didn't deliver Paul because he wasn't appropriating the grace of God already present in the provision made through the blood of Jesus. Entreating the Lord three times was like sitting in the airplane, begging the Lord for deliverance from gravity. The Lord would tell you, "Turn on the engine. Implement the law of aerodynamics already available for your deliverance."

This is what the Lord told Paul in verse nine. He told Paul, "My grace, (which has already been manifested in the law of life through the blood of Jesus) is sufficient for your deliverance." I don't believe God told Paul that His grace was sufficient for Paul to remain in satanic bondage. No! God does not work through Satan or the law of sin and death. God and Satan are not allies against you. Satan wants to destroy you through the law of sin and death, but God wants to give you victory through the law of life in Jesus.

I believe that in verse nine Paul was told by God that His grace through the blood of Jesus was already manifest to walk in. God's grace was sufficient — not for Paul to endure defeat by Satan, but for him to be delivered and come back into victory in the spirit. The Lord was saying that His power was to be manifest through Paul's spirit. In order for him to have victory, he would have to allow his own strength to become weak and die, and allow the power of Jesus in his spirit to become strong and gain preeminence in his soul.

In summary, Paul had allowed his flesh to gain preeminence in a certain area and, through it, was afflicted by a satanic messenger bent on Paul's destruction. He had tried to fight in the power of his own strength.

He probably used the truth of God as a law in his mind. Then, he begged the Lord for deliverance, but he wasn't delivered. Finally, the Lord reminded Paul, "You will always be defeated if you try to fight Satan and sin in your own strength and willpower." God said, "Quit trying to be strong and resist by your own strength. Allow your flesh to become weak and die. Begin to appropriate the power of the blood of Christ that is already resident in your born-again spirit."

It is so important that we learn to perceive in the spirit when God is revealing where sin has taken us captive through our flesh. We cannot afford to let flesh reign in any area, because Galatians 5:9 warns that "little leaven leavens the whole lump of dough."

What you may consider to be a "small area of fleshly domination" may be all that Satan needs to afflict you with something meant for your destruction. Remember, the nature of the flesh is the very nature of the same spirit who orchestrated the death of six million Jews in World War II and motivated Jim Jones and his followers to suicide. If you see sin in your flesh in that way, you will begin to hate it as God does and determine not to allow it to dominate you in even the smallest area. Proverbs 9:10 reveals that the true fear of the Lord is the beginning of wisdom, and Proverbs 8:13 says fear of the Lord is not being afraid of God, but is to hate evil as God hates it.

There are two opposing laws in which we can walk: the law of death, or the law of life in Jesus. We gain the freedom to choose Jesus' life through the following seven steps: (1) receive revelation knowledge from God of where your flesh may be operating supremely, unknown to you; (2) receive God's love in that area; (3) trust Him to meet your needs in that area and come into faith in Him; (4) repent of the sin He revealed to you; (5) receive God's forgiveness and the cleansing of the blood of Jesus Christ (I John 1:9); (6) acknowledge the truth of who you are in the spirit; (7) purpose to walk in the spirit in that area of your life.

Chapter Four:
Our True Image
In Christ

Ken had been born again for some years and felt that God was calling him into a singing ministry for Him. He had a beautiful voice and a wonderful talent for writing songs. However he wasn't sure whether God was really calling him into a music ministry, because, in his mind, Ken really felt that his voice was not very good, and that he didn't have the natural talent to sing. In fact, he wondered whether people would like his singing and thought that, at best, they would only be tolerant as an act of kindness.

As Ken shared his thoughts, I wondered where he had gotten the idea that his voice was not very good. I asked him, and he related to me the following story.

When he had been in college, Ken was very interested in music and enrolled in a voice class. In one of the first class meetings, the voice teacher asked each student to sing a short piece, and then the teacher would critique them to help them improve their voice quality. Ken had been the first one to stand up and sing. After he had finished, the voice teacher announced quite sarcastically, "Well, now you all have an example of how *not* to sing."

The teacher did not realize that when she spoke those words, she was prophesying into Ken's life. Ken heard those words and his faith in them began. He meditated on those words, and his faith in them grew stronger. The stronger his faith and confidence in the truth of those words became, the deeper his false self-image produced by those words became. As I shared with Ken that he really was believing in a false image of himself, he repented. He asked the Lord's forgiveness for putting his faith in a "graven image" instead of in God and what

He had spoken about his ministry. As he did so, the false image which had become a stronghold in his mind began to dissolve (2 Corinthians 10:3-5). The Blood of Jesus began to cleanse and renew Ken's mind to the truth. Essentially, he was terminating the effects of the law of sin and death in his life and beginning to operate the law of life in Jesus regarding his song ministry.

One of the primary ways that sin in our flesh works to deceive us is through false images of ourself, God, and others. If we put faith and trust in a false mental image, but we believe that it is true, then our flesh has free reign to operate in accordance with that image. Jesus said that when you receive the knowledge of the real truth, it will set you free. Words and experiences which come into our lives are seeds that either bind us in lies or free us in truth. When God created the earth, He created it with an inherent law that every living thing was to reproduce after its own kind. We see in Genesis 1:11 that every seed was created to bear fruit after its own kind, and that the seed of the next plant was in the fruit.

Then God said, "Let the earth sprout vegetation, plants yielding seed, and fruit trees bearing fruit after their kind, with seed in them, on the earth" and it was so (Genesis 1:11).

This means that if you plant an apple seed, it doesn't produce an orange tree. It produces an apple tree with fruit bearing more apple seeds. In verses 21 through 25 of Genesis 1, we see that God created all the birds and animals also to reproduce only after their own kind. In verses 26 and 27 God created man in His own image, (spirit, soul, and body) and made him to reproduce after his own kind.

Therefore, God has established that whatever kind of seed is planted, it will reproduce only after its own kind. Likewise, when we were born again, God planted a seed in our spirit. What is the nature of that seed?

"For you have been born again, not of seed which is perishable but imperishable, that is, through the living and abiding word of God" (1 Peter 1:23).

Who (not "what") is the living and abiding Word of God? John 1 tells you that in the beginning was the Word; the Word was with God and the Word was God. That Word became flesh, so it is evident that the Word of God is the Lord Jesus Christ. He bore fruit that contained a seed and was planted in your spirit when you were born again. That "seed" is imperishable and incorruptible. This is directly opposed, for example, to the natural human seed or male sperm which is very perishable. It lives for only a few short moments when exposed to the air. Many things can happen to that seed, causing it to die even after conception. But the seed of Jesus Christ in our spirit is not susceptible to other elements. It is pure, imperishable, and incorruptible.

That seed of Christ in your spirit has all the fullness of the nature and qualities of Jesus Christ. Because, like a seed, it can only reproduce after its own kind, John said that this seed cannot produce sin:

"No one who is born of God practices sin, because His seed abides in him; and he cannot sin, because he is born of God (I John 3:9).

Our spirit man cannot sin after we are born again. For that reason, Galatians 5:16 explains that if we walk in the spirit, it is impossible to carry out the desire of the flesh (sin). The truth of who you are in the spirit is that you are "everything" Jesus Christ was and is. In your spirit you have the power, character and authority of Jesus Christ. This was miraculously implanted in your spirit, in seed form, by God when you were born again. Paul calls this the "great mystery" that for years was hidden from the Gentiles.

"To whom God willed to make known what is the riches of the glory of this mystery among the Gentiles, which is Christ in you, the hope of glory" (Colossians 1:27).

When you were born again, the nature of your spirit man was miraculously changed, but your self-image (in your mind and emotions) probably remained primarily the same. You continued to perceive yourself in the same old way: through the same images that you had before you were born again. Some of us, of course, had dramatic changes in certain areas of our lives when we received Jesus. But even so, certain areas of our lives remained the same. These are the areas that need to be renewed by God's Word.

The truth is that, if you are born again, you are complete in Jesus Christ. Jesus is sufficient to meet all your needs (Colossians 2:6-10). You are wise, righteous, sanctified, and redeemed (I Corinthians 1:30), (2 Corinthians 5:21). You have the mind of Christ (I Corinthians 2:16). You are holy and blameless (Ephesians 1:4). You are a new creature (2 Corinthians 5:17). You truly are holy, because Jesus is holy in you (I Peter 1:16).

This is the way that God wants us to view ourselves. He doesn't want us to be "sin conscious." He wants us to be "righteousness conscious." We're not to identify ourselves with sin in our flesh, but we're to identify ourselves with the nature of Jesus in our spirit. This makes the fellowship of our faith effective.

"And I pray that the fellowship of your faith may become effective **through the knowledge of every good thing** *which is in you for Christ's sake" (Philemon 1:6).*

Make a commitment to identify yourself with your spirit, not your flesh. Don't agree with the what devil says about you. Begin to agree with what God says about you. Did you know that whatever you think about yourself, you will become? If you think a certain way about yourself, by continuing to think it, you will reinforce an image in your soul.

"For as he thinketh in his heart, **so is he:** *Eat and drink, saith he to thee; but his heart is not with thee" (Proverbs 23:7).*

Your human soul is like a camera that will form an image of that on which you focus. If you focus on your flesh, your self-image will be predominantly that of flesh. If you focus on the nature of Jesus Christ in your spirit, your self-image in your soul will become like His.

Sometimes when I have explained this to Christians, they have said, "You are asking me to tell lies about myself. I can't go around thinking and speaking lies about myself. That is just 'self deception.'"

I say, "No, it is not. It is beginning to put faith in God's truth about you instead of in your experience of yourself."

If you put more trust and confidence in the circumstances, people's words, your emotions, and your five senses, then you are deceived and are agreeing with the devil about yourself. You are letting your flesh determine your self-image by having trust in temporary surroundings rather than the eternal Word of God.

One day a woman came to my office for counseling for chronic depression. She began to tell me, "I know that, because of my particular temperament, I have a propensity toward depression." She had been seeing herself as a depressed person because she believed she was prone to it due to her temperament.

"Are you sure that you are born again? Is Jesus your Lord?" I asked her.

"Yes," she answered.

"What temperament does Jesus Christ have?" I then asked her.

"Well," she replied, "He must have all of the good qualities of each temperament."

I asked the woman if she thought that Jesus Christ was depressed.

"No," she answered. So I shared with her that she was born again of the imperishable seed of Jesus Christ.

"You have His nature already resident in your spirit," I assured, "and that nature has no propensity toward depression."

I pointed out that she didn't need to discover the negative tendencies of her flesh and then try to overcome them. This had only been making her more and more "flesh conscious" and not "spirit conscious". In doing this, the woman had identified with her flesh and tried to fight against it with her own willpower. She had used God's Word as a law in her mind.

Because of the deceptiveness of sin, and the theories and doctrines through which this woman perceived herself, she had difficulty seeing the sin of identifying with her flesh. Not seeing it, she could not repent of something that had not yet convicted her. She was placing faith in her experience of depression, not in the truth of who God said she is in the spirit.

Put simply, when we have faith and trust in circumstances or words that are contrary to God's Word, we are in sin and being ruled by our flesh. When the spies of Israel went into Canaan and returned to tell what they saw and experienced *in the flesh,* God called this an "evil report."

"When they returned from spying out the land, at the end of forty days, they proceeded to come to Moses and Aaron and to all the congregation of the sons of Israel in the wilderness of Paran, at Kadesh; and they brought back word to them and to all the congregation and showed them the fruit of the land. Thus they told him, and said, 'We went into the land where you sent us; and it certainly does flow with milk and honey, and this is its fruit. Nevertheless, the people who live in the land are strong, and the cities are fortified and very large; and moreover, we saw the descendants of Anak there. Amalek is living in the land of the Negev and the Hittites and the Jebusites and the Amorites are living in the hill country, and the Canaanites are living by the sea and by the side of Jordan.' Then Caleb quieted the people before Moses, and said 'We should by all means go up and take possession of it, for we shall surely overcome it.' But the men who had gone up with him said, 'We are not able to go up against the people, for they are too strong for us.' So they gave out to the sons of Israel a bad report of the land which they had spied out, saying, 'The land through which we have gone, in spying out, is a land that devours its inhabitants; and all the people whom we saw in it are men of great size. There also we saw the Nephilim (the sons of Anak are part of the Nephilim); and we became like grasshoppers in our own sight, and so were in their sight' " (Numbers 13:25-33).

The 10 spies did not tell any lies. They only explained what they had heard with their ears, had seen with their eyes, and experienced with their emotions. Then they drew a conclusion using natural reasoning; "We should not go up into the land, or we will be beaten in battle." God called this an evil report.

The two other spies saw, heard, and experienced the same thing as the 10. But they came to an entirely different conclusion: "We will win the battle!" The two spies' trust and confidence lay not in what they had seen or experienced.

Their trust lay in what God had said.

God had already told His people, "I will give you the land and victory."

The purpose of the spy trip was not made so that the spies would decide by five-sense knowledge whether to believe and obey what God had already said. The trip was made to determine the details and logistics of moving in God's Word.

Because the people decided to put more confidence in the apparent circumstances and human reasoning, they missed out on entering into the land at that time.

Verse 33 reveals a false self-image that the 10 spies formed of themselves as grasshoppers next to giants. They even thought that the enemy saw them as grasshoppers too. But the sons of Anak had undoubtedly heard of the God of Israel and the miracles He had performed in Egypt. They were very fearful of a people who fought in the power of a supernatural God! The 10 spies were not perceiving the truth in the spirit, but were agreeing with the devil about themselves, God, and the Canaanites. When we believe something about ourself that is contrary to what God says about us in the spirit, we are mocking God and agreeing with the devil.

One afternoon an irate husband whom I had been counseling called my home. I had counseled him and his wife the previous week. He told me that the following days had been the worst of his marriage. His wife was very depressed and was treating him terribly. Instead of improving, their marriage was becoming less stable each day. This, he claimed, was all due to my counseling.

"I don't know how you could represent yourself as a counselor, and I am not even sure that you are a Christian! Last week's session as the poorest example of any kind of counseling I have ever seen," he said. But he agreed to come in the next day for an appointment with me to discuss it further.

After I hung up the phone I was quite devastated. The next morning, as I drove to the church for counseling, I wondered whether God had really called me to be a counselor. I thought, "I'm probably a rotten counselor, I shouldn't try to counsel anyone else." To put it mildly, I felt like a poor counselor and horrible about myself in general.

Later in the day, I confided these thoughts to Jean Orr, who was at that time the director of New Life Counseling Center. Jean asked me, "Do the words that he spoke about you, or your emotions about those words, change the truth of who you really are in Christ Jesus?"

I thought about that for a moment, and then I said, "No, I suppose I'm still the same person in the Lord. My identity hasn't changed."

With those words, I suddenly saw how I had allowed the counselee's words and my feelings to create a false image in my mind about myself as a counselor. I repented of not perceiving in the spirit what God had to say about me and of not aligning my self-image with His Word. As it turned out, the man came in to see me in a very repentant and apologetic state. He had experienced an ugly disagreement with his wife and, in a state of rage, called me up and blamed me for it.

You can see that it is very important not to allow the words of others, or your natural interpretation of circumstances and experiences, to create a false self-image in you. Any self-image contrary to the truth of who God says you are in the spirit is a false self-image, so agree with God, not with your flesh or the devil.

I thought of how God told Gideon, in Judges 6:11-17, to deliver Israel from the Midianites, and Gideon argued with God according to his false self-image. He said, "I'm too young and my family members are nobodies here in Israel. If you want to use someone to deliver Israel, choose somebody from a valiant and noble family. If you must use my family, choose one of my older brothers, because I am neither worthy nor capable."

Many Christians feel this way about themselves: unworthy and incapable. But that is a *false* self-image, not an image from God. God continued to speak the truth to Gideon so persistently that he finally believed it and was used mightily to defeat a very large army with only 300 men! Likewise, an awareness of who Jesus is in you will cause you to defeat even the worst spiritual foes.

It's interesting to compare the initial image that Gideon had of himself with the self-image that David had when he was used by God to slay Goliath in I Samuel 17. David's trust and confidence was not in himself and his own ability, but in God. His personal identity rested in who he was in God — not who David was in the flesh. Gideon, on the other hand, was trusting in himself and not in God, because he wasn't convinced of God's love for him and was afraid of God. He interpreted the circumstances as saying, "God isn't faithful to meet our needs." At first, Gideon wouldn't believe God, because his identity was totally related to his flesh, while David's was totally related to God.

As with Gideon and David, God does not want us to identify with flesh. He wants us to crucify our flesh and live in our spirit (Romans 8:13). Did you know that when you believe and put your faith in a false image, you are actually believing in a *graven* image? Ponder this:

"You shall have no other Gods before me. You shall not make for yourself a graven image, or any likeness of anything that is in heaven above, or that is in the earth beneath, or that is in the water under the earth" (Exodus 20:3-4, King James Version).

Graven means "artificial," or "man-made." A graven

image is a false image that is man-made. The Lord often had to rebuke the Israelites for making and worshiping images of gods made from wood, metal or stone. This was idolatry and an abomination to God. When you, today, receive and put your faith in any image in your mind about God that is false, it is a graven image just as if you had created a physical image. God does not want us to worship Him through graven (man-made, false) images. Does He want us to relate to ourselves or others through those images? Graven images are abominable to God, and He hates them. Shouldn't we feel the same when we discover such in ourselves?

Where do false images about ourselves come from? I believe that the primary ways we develop false self-images are through our own human reasoning and interpretation of two things: (1) words we hear; and (2) experiences we have.

Look first at how words create false self-images. Romans 10:17 declares that "Faith comes from hearing, and hearing by the Word of Christ." Faith in Christ comes by hearing the Word of Christ. But it is also true that faith in someone else, or something else, can come by the hearing of someone else's words. Remember that words are seeds that bear fruit after their own kind. We hear words from people all day long, every day. Some of these words are true, and some are false. However, if we receive someone's word about us into our soul and begin to put faith in that word and believe it is true, that Word proceeds to form an image of ourselves in our minds and emotions. Whether true or false, it becomes true to us.

Since we were small children, people have been feeding us information about ourselves through words. Our parents tell us who we are when we're very small: "You're a good girl," or "You were naughty." Having no way to judge those words, most children receive and believe deep in their hearts the things that their parents say. If your parents told you that you weren't very smart, you probably considered yourself less intelligent than others.

You are probably just as intelligent as others, but because you have a false image of yourself, you see yourself that way.

Words that we receive about ourselves from others are actually "prophecy" to us. If we hear a word and receive it, begin to put faith in it, and form an image in our soul according to it, it will come to pass in our life. It is a prophecy. The Lord has warned us in His Word about receiving, or giving prophecy. The only words that we are to receive about ourselves are those from the Spirit of God in accordance with what He says is true of us in the spirit:

> *"Thus says the Lord of hosts, 'Do not listen to the words of the prophets who are prophesying to you. They are leading you into futility; They speak a vision **of their own imagination**, Not from the mouth of the Lord. They keep saying to those who despise Me, "The Lord has said, 'You will have peace'; and as for every one who walks in the stubbornness of his own heart, They say, 'Calamity will not come upon you.' But who has stood in the council of the Lord, That he should **see** and **hear** His word? Who has given heed to His word and listened?" (Jeremiah 23:16-18).*

We are to stand in the counsel of the Lord to first hear and then see (form a correct image of) His Word. If someone speaks a word to you that is not in accordance with God's Word, don't receive it — even if the word is in accord with your flesh, or with circumstances. It is not the truth of who you really are. By the same token, weigh cautiously the words you speak to others, particularly your children, spouse, or parents. You don't want to be a false prophet agreeing with the devil. Instead, be a true prophet and agree with God by planting seeds of truth in your loved ones' souls.

A second way that we form false self-images is through wrong interpretation of circumstances and experiences that we perceive with our five senses and emotions. This is what happened to the 10 Israeli spies in Numbers 13. They interpreted their experiences wrongly according to human reasoning and drew a conclusion that led them to a false image of themselves. They perceived themselves as grasshoppers next to giants. In doing so they received a graven image rather than God's image for their situation. When they spoke that falsehood from their mouths, they uttered a false prophecy over their nation, which in the end, brought bitter results.

Once we form a false self-image, we also form an expectation about our lives. Have you ever wondered why some people seem to always have things go wrong in their lives, or why others who are no more wealthy, intelligent, or talented seem to have a blessed, fulfilling life? This is only because the first person experiences his life to be negative through false images and false expectations arising from those images. Every one of us operates in false images in certain areas. However, as we open ourselves to the spirit of God and allow Him to reveal those areas to us, we can tear them down by the power of the blood of Jesus and enter into truth.

In 1863, a federal law was passed in the United States outlawing slavery. That law made it illegal for one man to own another as property. In terms of legal status, the day after that law was enacted, every slave in the U.S. was a free man. However, years later many were still living as slaves. They were not exercising their rights and authority as free men. They were still subject to the bondage of slavery to their white masters. Why was this? One reason was because some authorities were unjust and didn't properly and righteously enforce the law. But a greater reason was due to false self-images ingrained in the minds of the blacks themselves. They had been slaves all their lives, so the only personal identity they had ever known was that of being slaves.

Suppose a black man who had been a slave all his life was suddenly told, "You are free," and he began to contemplate his freedom. Perhaps he would think, "If I don't live here, where will I live? Where will I work? How will I make a living? What if nobody will hire me? I and my family will perish."

You can imagine the fear that overwhelmed such a

man, as he pondered all the unknowns of freedom. Perhaps he would conclude that it was safer to stay a slave. Many did just that. You say, "But what if the master continues to treat the slave cruelly?" Often, fears of the free world's unknowns were so intense that they just tolerated cruel security. Their images of themselves were of being in slavery. Such images kept them in bondage.

This analogy is similar to the state of born-again Christians in certain soulish bondage. Romans 6:6-7 declares that we are no longer slaves to sin, but free from it. Furthermore, Romans 8:2 says the law of life in Jesus *has* (past tense) set us free from the law of death. The primary reason for walking in the flesh is because sin in our flesh has deceived us. For that reason, we are like a freed slave in 1865, continuing to accept bondage and cruelty. Because of a false image, we fail to be convinced that we can be freed from the devil or our flesh.

Once we hear a word or interpret an experience, we have a choice: whether to receive that image as truth or reject it as false. If we perceive what God says in the spirit and weigh it with His Word, we will draw correct conclusions. However, if we reason about it in our natural minds, we will receive a wrong image. Unfortunately, it does not stop there. Once we receive a false image and call it the truth, we begin to put faith in it. This image generates a wrong expectation through which we filter future words and experiences. Thus, the validity of our initial false images are confirmed. Years and years of such confirmation ingrains these images deeply in our souls and makes them difficult to uproot.

Not only are we put down by false images, however, but they also hurt our relationship with God. Anytime that we operate in the flesh and not in the spirit, we are hardening our heart in that direction. The Bible tells us that when we do this, even unwittingly, we exclude ourselves from the life of God in that area:

"Being darkened in their understanding, excluded from the life of God, because of the ignorance that is in them, because of the hardness of their heart" (Ephesians 4:18).

How then are we to view ourselves? Only as the new creatures that we are in our born-again spirits. We do so by allowing God to reveal where we have agreed with the devil about ourselves so we can repent and begin to agree with God:

*"Therefore, from now on **we recognize no man according to the flesh;** even though we have known Christ according to the flesh, yet now we know Him thus no longer. Therefore, if any man is in Christ, he is a new creature; the old things passed away; behold, new things have come" (2 Corinthians 5:16-17).*

If you view yourself as you are in the spirit, you can also view others the very same way. Paul said that you are to recognize *no man* according to the flesh. In other words, "See every born-again believer as they truly are in the spirit and relate to them that way. Even when someone is behaving in the flesh, you are not to recognize them as such. Don't speak to or about them as being that way, or even think of them that way, because the Word says for you to acknowledge the spirit.

This being true, how should you view an unbeliever? His spirit is unredeemed and still has the same nature as his flesh. Obviously, you can't view him according to his spirit, because he is unredeemed. The key is to view unbelievers as Jesus does:

"And He will delight in the fear of the Lord, and He will not judge by what His eyes see, Nor make a decision by what His ears hear" (Isaiah 11:3).

Jesus never judges or draws conclusions according to His five senses. Rather, Jesus always sees people in an attitude of love. Love doesn't see people in the flesh, but always sees them with redemptive vision. Therefore, this is how we're to see others:

"For I determined to know nothing among you except Jesus Christ, and Him crucified" (I Corinthians 2:2).

The Greek word translated "among"[1] in the above verse actually means, "in, within, or about." Paul was actually saying he'd determined to know nothing about the Corinthians except Jesus Christ and Him crucified. Even though Paul had to rebuke the Corinthians, he did so in love, and refused to know them "after the flesh."

Your mind will immediately tell you, "If you begin to treat others this way, by doing so, they will take advantage of you and walk all over you!" The idea is that you must keep your defenses up against their flesh, or you will be hurt. Your mind will tell you that a better way to help someone change is to point out their problems so that they can repent. In truth, this is exactly the opposite of what the Bible instructs. By pointing out people's faults, you are identifying them by their flesh and helping them identify with their flesh. (I'm not talking about a counseling situation, but a relationship).

Jesus tells us that changes come to circumstances and relationships this way: through prayer and asking the Father, and then believing and acting as though we have already received that for which we've prayed. This is the mechanism by which our prayers come to pass:

*"Truly I say to you, whoever says to this mountain 'be taken up and cast into the sea,' and does not doubt in his heart, but believes that what he says is going to happen, it shall be granted him. Therefore, I say to you, all things for which you pray and ask, **believe that you have received them,** and they shall be granted you" (Mark 11:23-24).*

Perhaps your spouse or child have areas in their lives that look insurmountable to you. Stop agreeing with the devil about your loved ones. Don't foster a false image in them by relating to them as if the problem area were still there. Even if you see the problem before your eyes, don't put your faith in it. Put your faith in God by believing that you have received that for which you've prayed: a change in your loved one.

God's principle is for you to call into being things that are true, but are yet unmanifest in the natural. A born-again person has all the fullness of Jesus Christ dwelling in his spirit in seed form. However, it may not yet all be manifest in his soul life. To see a change in someone, view him in the spirit and call into being the things which don't yet exist in the natural but are already present in the supernatural in his spirit — the character of Jesus.

*"As it is written, A father of many nations have I made you in the sight of Him whom he believed, even God, **who gives life to the dead and calls into being that which does not exist**" (Romans 4:17).*

The mechanism through which we receive that for which we have prayed is to believe that we have already received it. We call it so with our mouth, and act as if it were already so. Don't speak and call for that which you already have. You do not need that! Call for what you do not have. If your husband is often angry, or your wife moody, don't view and speak to him or her about the negatives. That simply strengthens the image in you and in them of the negative traits. Why call for more anger and moodiness? You already have anger and moodiness. Instead, call for peace, joy, and life in the spirit.

The best analogy we can use to understand this principle is that of pregnancy. Anytime after conception, a mother can truthfully say, "I have a baby," but it is not physically manifest in fullness until birth. When we speak the Word of God forth into a circumstance, our life, or someone else's life, we are planting a seed and conception has occurred. During the ensuing time of pregnancy, we simply continue to believe that we have received that for which we have prayed. When a birth then occurs, we see manifest in the natural that for which we have prayed. Thus, we want our words to agree with the truth in the spirit, not the manifestation in the soul.

"For by your words will you be justified, and by your words you will be condemned" (Matthew 12:37).

"Death and life are in the power of the tongue. And those who love it will eat its fruit" (Proverbs 18:21).

Make sure your tongue always speaks forth life, not death, to and about others. You can only do this by walking in the spirit yourself and allowing the nature of Jesus Christ in your spirit to fill your soul.

In Matthew 12:34, Jesus said that your mouth speaks from whatever fills your heart. If your heart is full of the love and life of Jesus Christ, your mouth will automatically speak words of love and life. If it is full of flesh and death, your mouth will speak that forth. Don't just use the Word as a law by seeking to control your words with human willpower. If you find fleshly words coming out of your mouth about someone else; let that be an indication to you that your flesh is dominant in that area. Ask yourself whether you are trusting God in your relationship with that person, and go to God in prayer. He will help you perceive in the spirit and be convicted of sin in your flesh. Then you can repent and be cleansed by the blood, thereby activating the law of life in you.

I once visited a Polish-speaking couple for help in translating something that I needed to send to friends in Poland. I told my wife, Jan, "I'll only be gone for an hour." While I was there, however, the couple heard that I was involved in Christian counseling and asked me to counsel them regarding a situation in their lives. Almost four hours later, I called Jan to let her know that I was late and was just leaving for home. But, I detected she was angry with me — that our two-year-old son, Joshua, had been naughty and hard to take care of, and she felt I should have been there to help.

As I got into the car to drive home, I felt terrible. Death had come into my soul, and I was not looking forward to going home. I had experienced this situation before, and that mood would usually last in Jan all evening once it had began. Feeling guilty, I would compensate by very busily trying to "atone" for my offense by taking care of Josh, speaking kindly, doing as many household chores as possible and trying to appease Jan's flesh. That never worked, and our relationship usually remained cool all evening.

That evening as I drove home I prayed in the spirit, and the Lord spoke to me, "Begin to call forth in prayer the truth of who Jan is in the spirit." I began to pray, "Thank you, Lord, that Jan is redeemed from the law of sin and death. I say in the name of Jesus Christ that she walks in the spirit and not in the flesh. Thank you, Lord, that Jan is full of life, peace, joy and forgiveness."

Then the Holy Spirit said, "You are just confessing words. You still see your wife in the flesh. You expect that when you get home, she'll be angry all evening, because that is how it has been in the past. You are still seeing an image of death." The Lord showed me that I was like a pilot sitting in a plane and confessing flight in prayer, but not turning on the engine to operate the law of aerodynamics.

I repented of viewing Jan in the flesh and putting trust in what I had heard with my ears. I decided to go ahead and believe that I had already received that for which I had prayed. I determined that when I got home, no matter what the circumstances were, or what words she said to me, I would know and recognize nothing in her except "Jesus Christ and Him crucified." God had told me, "Act as though she were in the spirit, even if she behaves in the flesh."

When I got home, Jan was still frustrated and angry with me. God had convicted me that I had stayed too long and had dishonored Jan by not calling her much earlier. Upon seeing Jan, I first confessed the wrong and asked for her forgiveness. She said that she forgave me, but I could still sense her anger. Then, instead of trying to appease her and cater to her flesh, I continued to speak and relate to Jan as though she were being dominated by her spirit. (It was difficult, because her flesh was inciting and antagonizing mine!) However, I had already determined to know *nothing* within her but Jesus Christ in her spirit.

After approximately 20 minutes, the entire mood had lifted and Jan was back living in the spirit. I was amazed myself because every time before her moods had lasted all evening. Indeed, the law of the spirit of life in Christ Jesus has already set us free from the law of sin and death. Only false images that we have of God, ourselves, and others cause us to fall short of the law of life in Jesus.

Many times I have heard Christians say that we need to "get the Bible knowledge we have from our head down into our hearts." But I don't believe that our intellectual knowledge of the Word needs to go anywhere. What we need is to get our minds, wills, and emotions renewed by the power of the Holy Spirit and the washing of the water of the Word (Ephesians 5:26) to the truth of who we already are in the spirit. Our souls are what must be renewed with the knowledge of our identity in the spirit. We don't need to get our spirits renewed with intellectual understanding of the Bible, but to get our minds renewed to the truth of what God has already done in our spirits. God is not trying to change our identity in the spirit. He is only trying to help us walk in our true identity of who we *already are* in the spirit. Our spirits are already redeemed, free from the law of sin and death, holy, righteous, and pure.

When Jesus told the Jews, "You shall know the truth and the truth shall make you free," they answered Him; "We are Abraham's offspring, and have never yet been enslaved to anyone; how is it that You say; You shall become free" (John 8:32-33). They didn't recognize their bondage, because of false images through which they viewed God, themselves and sin.

To stop such images and gain a new image, we need to allow the Holy Spirit to reveal false images of ourselves, God, and others in our minds. Otherwise, like the Jews, we will remain in bondage and won't come into knowledge of the truth:

"And do not be conformed to this world, but be transformed by the renewing of your mind, that you may prove what the will of God is, that which is good and acceptable and perfect" (Romans 12:2).

Let's get our minds renewed to the truth in our spirits. When God reveals a false image, a fleshly stronghold in your mind, tear it down through repentance and acknowledging the truth of God within your spirit.

*"For though we walk in the flesh, we do not war after the flesh; (for the weapons of our warfare are not carnal, but mighty through God to the **pulling down of strongholds**;) Casting down imaginations, and every high thing that exalteth itself against the knowledge of God, and bringing into captivity every thought to the obedience of Christ"* *(2 Corinthians 10:3-5, KJV).*

As you tear down false images and begin to walk in the true identity of your spirit, the incorruptible seed of life in your spirit will bear fruit after its own kind, and that fruit will become manifest in every area of your life.

1. James Strong, "The Exhaustive Concordance of the Bible," Abingdon Press, New York, 1890, pp.63, pp.28 Greek dictionary.

Chapter Five:
Superficial Manifestations
Of The Flesh

Our flesh utilizes four powerful instruments to keep us in bondage to the law of sin and death. These are: 1) bitter root judgment, 2) false expectations stemming from judgment, 3) false expectations based on false self-image, and 4) manipulation.

The first initial judgment of another person causes a root of bitterness to spring up. Proceeding forth from that root of bitterness, however, comes not just one, but many subsequent judgments. These bitter root judgments are based upon false images established in the soul. Such images motivate us to unwittingly walk in the flesh even after we are born again.

"See to it that no one comes short of the grace of God; that **no root of bitterness** *springing up causes trouble, and by it many be defiled" (Hebrews 12:15).*

The type of judgment here should not be confused with spiritual discernment. To have a bitter root judgment means to draw a negative conclusion about the character of another person, especially someone in relationship to you. These conclusions are based on your assessment of their attitude, words and behavior toward you, which causes you to judge the person. The Bible, however, tells us not to judge people in such a manner.

God's Word tells us not to judge, because judgment is an indicator that we already have, or will, take on the very same root attitude that we are judging in others.

You say, "If I judge a homosexual, will I become a homosexual?" Perhaps not; however, you will open yourself up to be controlled by your flesh in the weakest area of your life. Judgment also has the ability to reproduce, in the lives of others close to you, the same fleshly attitudes and behaviors that you have judged in others.

How many women complain that their husbands treat them just like their fathers once did? Or men whose wives treat them just like their mothers? This hasn't happened by accident. These husbands and wives have — through the deceitfulness of sin through judgment — created these behavioral patterns or attitudes in their spouses.

Judgment works this way, as it creates in you a false image of other people and yourself in relationship to them. These false images are seeds planted in the soul: they reproduce after their own kind according to the law of sowing and reaping.

"Do not be deceived. God is not mocked; for whatever a man sows, this he will also reap. For the one who sows to his own flesh shall from the flesh reap corruption but the one who sows to the spirit shall from the Spirit reap eternal life" (Gal. 6:7-8).

One aspect of the law of sowing and reaping is that you always reap more than you sow. Any farmer knows that if you sow one seed, it will yield a plant with many fruits, each fruit often containing many new seeds. When you judge, the false images that you form of yourself, and others, become an emotional focus in your soul. Remember, your soul is like a camera, producing in your life that on which it focuses. Judgment focuses the soul wrongly through negative false images which results in reaping bad fruit.

I have a minister friend, Steve, who is powerfully used of God in preaching, teaching, and counseling. However, sometime ago, the Lord revealed to Steve how certain bitter root judgments were diminishing the effectiveness of his ministry and destroying his personal life and family. Steve had grown up as a boy in a poor urban neighborhood. He didn't like being poor, and, even worse, he considered his father to be lazy and tolerant of their bad situation. He didn't seem to want to change it. Steve judged his father for being lazy and not trying to change the situation for his family. Further, Steve vowed that he would never be like his dad. But Steve's judgments did not end at home. He judged bureaucrats in the government, and society for being insensitive to the needs of the poor.

As Steve grew up to be a young man, he became very militant and joined a radical terrorist group in an attempt to do something about the plight of America's urban poor. While in this radical group, by the grace of God, Steve was born again, quit the group and began to live his life for Jesus Christ. However, these judgments continued to work death in and through him, without his conscious awareness or consent.

The two primary judgments working in Steve were related to laziness and insensitivity to the needs of others. Since being saved, however, instead of the judgments being eliminated, many more seeds of judgment had been reproduced and sown. Steve was now judging many other Christians and ministries whom he saw as either lazy or insensitive to people's needs. The end result was that he strove to be diligent in his work for the Lord, have compassion, and be sensitive to the needs of others. In doing so, he was sometimes unknowingly, and at other times consciously, comparing himself and his ministry with other ministries. Of course he always felt that he was a harder worker and more sensitive than anyone else. This self-image was emanating from pride in his flesh and not from the nature of Christ in his spirit. However, he thought his attitude was godly, because the judgment had blinded him in that area, so that sin (pride) in his flesh could deceive him. This is what Jesus referred to as having a "log" in one's eye.

"Do not judge lest you be judged yourselves. For in the way you judge, you will be judged; and by your standard of measure, it shall be measured to you. And why do you look at the speck in your brother's eye, but do not notice the log that is in your own eye? Or how can you say to your brother, 'Let me take the speck out of your eye,' and behold, the log is in your own eye? You

*hypocrite, first take the log out of your own eye, and then you will
see clearly enough to take the speck out of your brother's eye"
(Matthew 7:1-5).*

The problem is that, when you have a log in your
eye, you are deceived by sin, and you don't know it.
Steve had been preaching, counseling and ministering to
others 12-14 hours a day because he didn't want to be
found lazy or ineffective for the Lord. However, he was
always late for all of his appointments and rarely came
home at the time he had told his wife that he would.

As Steve's marriage began to deteriorate, his ministry effectiveness was diminished. Finally, in desperation, he sought Christian counseling and was surprised
to findhis wife's chief complaint was that he was insensitive to her needs and desires, and to those of the children, because he was always so busy ministering. Amazing! The root attitude and behavior that Steve had judged
in others, he developed toward his own family.

Sin in Steve's flesh working through judgment had
deceived him into practicing toward those whom he
loved the very thing he despised, hated and had judged
in others. Also, because much of his ministry was rooted
in pride, he had exalted himself through comparisons
with others whom he viewed as far more ineffective,
lazy, or insensitive. Thus, his ministry was far less
effective than it could have been, because he had not
been operating in the spirit. Steve was a man of God,
however, deeply committed to God's purposes in his
life, and when the Spirit of God revealed these things to
him, he repented and began to allow the Word to renew
his mind, and the truth to set him free. When we judge
another, a mechanism that begins within causes us to
purpose *not* to be like the person we have judged. This
very act allows sin in our flesh to deceive us into
becoming like the very thing we've judged in others —
usually in some other area of our lives that we haven't
seen. This is why the Bible tells us not to judge anyone,
ever. We cannot afford it!

Another mechanism operating through judgment for our destruction is that of future expectations. We expect similar behavior from others that is consistent with false images that we have received in judgment. Hebrews 12:15 tells us that, through the bitter root of judgment, *many* people are defiled. This expectation occurs as follows: When we judge, we form a false image of the person whom we judge as being a certain way and relating to us in a certain way. Then, because of this image, we expect others in the future to be the same way, and treat us the same as the person whom we judged.

For example, if a person of a different race acted unkindly toward you, you might then expect other people of his race would treat you the same unkind way. The world calls this prejudice. The Bible just calls it sin.

What if, for example, you judged your father for treating you a certain way? If you remained in that judgment, you would expect certain others, perhaps your husband, employer, commanding officer, or ultimately God, to treat you as your father had.

This expectation is easiest to see in a marriage relationship. Men often create in their wives the qualities that they judged in their mothers, and women will create in their husbands the qualities that they judged in their fathers. Consequently, men will tend to take on the qualities they judged in their fathers, and women their mothers. Have you ever wondered why your wife is just like her mother in certain negative qualities? It is because she judged her in those areas. Have you ever wondered why your husband is treating you just like he treats his mother? It's because he expects you to act like his mother in the areas he judged her.

Remember Terry who had difficulty hearing from God? In that counseling session, we didn't discuss Terry's judgment of her parents, but based on the current effects in her life, I imagine that she had judged her father for making her feel unimportant. When she grew up, she then expected that other men whom she might date or consider marrying would treat her the same way.

For example, when she began to date a man, a scenario similar to the following would ensue: She expected that he would ultimately reject her because she thought that she was really unimportant and of little value. She would be initially attracted to a man because he treated her with honor and esteem, as though she were valuable. But nonetheless, she expected that, sooner or later, he would find out the "truth" of how unimportant and worthless she really was and finally reject her.

Because of her false image, Terry had interpreted men's words, body language, and actions according to her false expectation of rejection, even though no such thinking was present in them at all. She then would begin to act defensively and accuse them of not really caring for her.

The men, at this point, would become totally baffled, wondering what had caused Terry to feel rejected. As time progressed in any given relationship, Terry misinterpreted words and actions according to her false expectation. Eventually, the man would become frustrated and on edge. Up until this point, he had felt only love and esteem for Terry. But finally that love dissipated to rejection. Can you see how the seed of hurt in Terry was powerfully at work, creating in men close to her the very attitudes she had hated in her father?

All along, Terry had prayed and asked God to help her in a relationship and give her a husband. Now she had been rejected, and she saw God through the same false image by which she saw the man whom she dated. This image of self and God still stems from Terry's judgment of her father. Because of her circumstances, it was confirmed to her (as she expected all along) that God didn't really like her, and that she was very unimportant and of not much value to Him too. To Terry, her circumstances bore witness to the truth of her expectations: "If God really loved me and thought that I was important, or of value, He would give me a husband. He could have helped me in this relationship but He didn't, so He obviously doesn't care."

The sin of false expectations had deceived Terry based on false images established in her soul through judgment of her father. This expectation damaged her relationship with God and kept her from receiving the husband and other good things that her loving heavenly Father desperately longed for her to have. So the past specific judgment of Terry's father created in her an expectation of how men, in general, would treat her in the present and future. This is the mechanism by which, through one bitter root of judgment, many are defiled (Hebrews 12:15).

Look at another example. Suppose a boy grows up with a mother who is obese, and he judges her for it. Now suppose there's a girl who grows up with a father whom she could never please, who was always critical of her, and she judges him for it. Let's say this young man and young woman decide to get married.

At first, everything starts out fine. The man was attracted to this young woman because she was beautiful and skinny, unlike his mother. The young woman was attracted to this fellow because he was kind, sensitive, and pleased with her, unlike her father. He never criticized her, because she was beautiful and everything that he wanted in a wife.

Neither of them had conscious expectations of one another, but unconsciously imprinted in their souls are false images with expectations arising out of judgment. He unconsciously expects women in his life to be fat. She unconsciously expects men in her life to be critical. Probably he had some fat women school teachers while growing up to help confirm the image, and she had some critical men teachers or employers.

Perhaps after a short time of marriage, hubby notices that his wife has gained a few pounds since they were married. In her efforts to be a good wife and please him, she has been cooking meals that are a little richer than might be in good order for her to maintain her figure. Immediately, because of his expectation and image, he becomes alarmed that his wife is getting a little overweight. She has actually gained only four pounds, but to him, he sees the one thing he couldn't tolerate in a wife coming to pass. So he approaches her about it as delicately as he can: "Honey, I have noticed that you have put on a few pounds. Perhaps we should join in a health club together."

That's not a terrible, critical comment. But, because of his wife's expectation and image, she becomes deeply concerned, "He's never criticized me before!" The one thing that she could not tolerate in a husband is coming to pass. She continues to think and meditate on that criticism and becomes worried about it. So she begins to do what many women do when they're worried or nervous: she begins to snack between meals.

As a result of the extra snacking, the wife gains a few more pounds, and this really worries her husband. He thinks, "Maybe I didn't speak to her strongly enough last time. Perhaps she doesn't understand how very important her figure and beauty are to me." So, as sweetly as possible, but a bit more strongly this time, he expresses his concern about her weight.

Her reaction to his criticism, of course, is more tension and stress resulting in more eating. You can see that soon he, through his expectation, has created a fat wife, and she through hers, a critical husband.

Perhaps this couple finally decides that they must have made a mistake in marrying one another. They each think, "My spouse was not really the person whom I thought that I married." No! The truth is they changed each other through their bitter root expectations. If this couple now divorces and marries other people, they will simply start the process all over again.

Bitter root judgment happens inevitably with every one of us in the areas where we have judged others. This is why the Bible is so adamant about not judging anyone, especially not our parents.

"Honor your father and your mother, as the Lord your God has commanded you, that your days may be prolonged, and that it

may go well with you on the land which the Lord your God gives you" (Deuteronomy 5:16).

If you judge your parents in any area of your life, that area of your life will not go well with you, and your days will not be prolonged in the land. You will be constantly reaping the consequences of the law of sin and death and not know why. So you may say, "God is teaching me something through this relationship," or "The devil is attacking me." Or you will be just plain frustrated and exasperated, certain that your problem is due completely to another person.

Know that, in most cases, you're drawing that behavior out of someone through your expectation. If you are having trouble with how your marriage partner, employer, friends, or others are treating you, it is probably due to your judgment, false images, and false expectations. Also, you are probably unknowingly viewing God in the same way. You may not believe that immediately, but the Word says it, and the Holy Spirit will show it to you if you're open to Him.

"If some one says, 'I love God,' and hates his brother, he is a liar; for the one who does not love his brother whom he has seen, cannot love God whom he has not seen" (I John 4:20).

The Scripture says that if you judge someone, you are not loving them. Therefore, you're hating them. (There's no in between!) This Scripture says when you judge, you are seeing God through the same image too. It surprises some people to find out that the way they relate to and respond to their marriage partner sexually is the same way they view them overall and is actually the same image through which they are viewing God.

Terry, whom I had counseled, was ultimately hating her father in judgment, and subsequently, hating the men she had dated, men in general, and ultimately God by seeing Him through the same false image. Do you see why judgment of others is so dangerous?

Another form of false expectation *doesn't* necessarily always arise out of judgment but is just as destructive. It comes from false images in our souls that have been deposited in other ways. This false expectation entails our wrongly endowing others with the same attitude about us as we have about ourselves.

This form of expectation is tied very closely to the other form. Usually they go hand in hand with one another. For example, Terry wanted to get married. But not only did she expect the man she dated to treat her as her father had, but she also expected him to think about her in the same way as she thought about herself.

For example, if I see myself as having a long nose, I will expect that everyone else sees and knows what a long nose I have. If I believe I am less intelligent that others, then, when I have a job interview, I will believe that the interviewer immediately recognizes my lack of intelligence. The truth is, however, that the interviewer has not yet formed an opinion about me and knows nothing about me. Because I see myself through a false image of being stupid, and I am certain that the interviewer sees me as stupid, I will lack confidence and consequently act stupid. The interviewer will then see me acting as if I were stupid, form an opinion that I must not be very bright, and treat me according to that opinion.

Once again, I have created my world to be consistent with my false self-image through false expectation. Now, when the interviewer treats me as stupid, my false self-image is strengthened and it confirms to me that, in truth, I must not be very intelligent.

This is the mechanism through which our flesh operates. False self-images in our souls draw behavior (not theretofore present) out of others that confirms to us the "truth" of a false image in which we believe.

Suppose a small child grows up with parents who don't discipline him properly. Instead of taking disciplinary action, the parents just yell and scream at the child, and he continues being disobedient. The parents constantly tell the child and others how naughty and disobedient he is.

When the child goes to first grade, the teacher doesn't know any of the children or anything about them. However, this little boy has an image of himself already ingrained in his soul: "I am a naughty, undisciplined boy." He also believes that all other adults around him already know that and believe that about him too.

The first day of school the boy goes to class and expects the teacher to treat him as naughty and disobedient. He, in his own mind, endows her with his own thoughts about himself. He acts naughty and disobedient — and wonder of wonders — the teacher treats him as a naughty, disobedient child! This confirms to him the truth of his image. The truth is that his flesh drew that behavior out of her and caused her to confirm to him his own false self-image. This is the mechanism by which our flesh manipulates the flesh of others to get them to confirm to us the false self-image in which we're walking.

Both of the previously discussed types of false expectations are used of the devil to keep you and others close to you in bondage to the false self-images that have been ingrained in your mind and emotions by sin in your flesh. The first type of false expectation is designed primarily to keep others around you in bondage to the images of past relationships through which you see them.

For example, suppose the man who had judged his mother for obesity suddenly had revelation of his judgment and of viewing his mother and wife after the flesh, not the spirit. Suppose that the Lord also convicted him that he was trying, through the strength and wisdom of his own flesh, to manipulate his wife through "sweet suggestions" (criticism) to get her to control her weight instead of viewing her in the spirit and calling into being that which doesn't yet exist, and believing and receiving that for which he'd prayed (Romans 4:17, Mark 11:24). Suppose the young man confesses all this to his wife, repents, and begins to walk in the spirit.

The wife, however, doesn't yet see her judgment, false expectation and false image. She continues to expect the husband to be critical despite his repentance.

This negative spiritual law will still operate through her attempting to draw criticism out of her husband toward her. If he continues to walk in the spirit, it can't be manipulated by her flesh. Flesh in one person can only create behavior eminating from flesh in another person.

However, because of her false image and expectation, she is not letting him change. She is unwittingly doing everything possible to make him conform to her image and be critical toward her.

If the husband yields to his spirit, he will go ahead and change anyway, regardless of whether his wife decides to view him in the spirit. But the wife, through not releasing her husband and viewing him in the spirit, makes it substantially harder for him to live in the truth of who he is in Christ. Essentially, the wife's fleshly attitudes are working overtime against the very desire of her heart: her desire to have a husband who doesn't criticize her. This is the way in which the first type of false expectations work to keep others in two types of bondage to their flesh and also our false images of them.

The second type of false expectation keeps us in bondage to our own false self-images. This mechanism causes others to view us the way we view ourselves. Once that image is established with others, they believe our false images about ourselves and won't release us from those images if we later repent.

If you believe that you are stupid, then through false expectations you might convince your employer that you are stupid. Later, however, you might gain knowledge of the truth of Jesus Christ (who isn't stupid) in your spirit. Thus, you would repent of walking in the flesh under the deception of sin. Your boss, however, might still continue treating you as though you were stupid because of his image of you (which your flesh created, by the way).

Walking in your true image in the spirit becomes much more difficult when others remind and treat you according to their old, false images of you.

A fourth area in which our flesh operates is through

the manipulation of others for the purpose of accomplishing our goals. This entails using whatever methods or words our flesh deems necessary to get another person to do what we want them to do.

The most common example is that of a Christian husband using a Bible study with his wife on submission (Ephesians 5) to convince his wife to agree with him on some point. Perhaps the wife is also trying to get the husband to do something for her. Because he is not complying, she withdraws sexually from him. The husband promptly reads I Corinthians 7 about how the wife's body is "not her own," but her husband's. Thus, the husband is not loving his wife, but is instead using God's Word to manipulate her.

This is an example of each person using fleshly manipulation in attempts to get one's own way. Chances are, right now you are either manipulating someone, or are being manipulated. It's happening in an area of your life where your flesh is exerting its preeminence, and you're probably unaware of it. You cannot be manipulated in any area where your spirit is preeminent, and your spirit won't lead you to manipulate others because your spirit leads you to trust in God to accomplish your purpose.

Fleshly manipulation, as I mentioned in an earlier chapter, can be very subtle. We can even use God's Word in the flesh to manipulate someone to give money to the church, receive Jesus, get baptized in the Holy Spirit, or repent of sin. These are all noble and right goals, but if we don't trust God to anoint His Word and convict people by His Spirit, we fall easily into this trap of manipulation in the flesh.

The scribes and Pharisees in Jesus' time tried constantly to manipulate Jesus for their own purposes. They were always trying to trap Him in the flesh or manipulate Him to conform to their doctrines and false images of holiness.

Jesus, however, was never manipulated. He always responded in the spirit. A born-again spirit cannot be manipulated by flesh, neither will it seek to manipulate others.

Manipulation is rooted in a false image of God as being unfaithful or unable to meet our needs or accomplish His purposes in our lives.

As a consequence of not having received God's love in this area, thus not trusting in God, our minds, governed by flesh, devise plans to accomplish our goals through manipulation.

Manipulation can be a very dangerous thing. In 2 Samuel 13:1-19 a young man, Amnon, destroyed the entire life of his sister, Tamar, through manipulating her to meet his needs and accomplish his purposes.

If God is convicting you of manipulating someone else, repent of not having trusted God and allowing your flesh to rule in that area. If you are being manipulated by someone, repent of having lived in the flesh, and determine to walk in the spirit. Remember, your recreated spirit has the nature of Jesus Christ and cannot be manipulated by anyone.

These are some of the mechanisms and techniques that our flesh uses to capture our souls and bring us into captivity to the law of death in our lives and in relationships with others. Take some time to seek God and allow Him to reveal to you, in the spirit, judgments, false expectations, false images, and manipulation. When you see such, don't despair, but rejoice in the goodness of God. Know its not *you,* but sin in your flesh operating illegally through you. Repent, be cleansed by the blood, and come into the knowledge of the truth. Walk in the spirit, and be holy for He (in you) is holy.

Chapter Six:
The Lion, The Bear and The Serpent

Perhaps, in reading these last few chapters, you have been convicted of bitter root judgments, manipulation and other manifestations of fleshly domination in your life. These are areas where sin in your flesh has deceived you through false images and taken you captive to the law of sin and death. However, these manifestations of fleshly preeminence are not simply isolated, unrelated events. Judgment, false expectations, and manipulation are merely superficial manifestations of an entire mode of operation of your flesh which has probably been present in your life since early childhood.

Judgment, false expectation, and manipulation are simply tips of an iceberg that first become visible to us in the spirit. The Lord doesn't want us to stop with the tip of the iceberg, but instead to reveal the entire system of deception causomg the judgments, manipulation, and other superficial manifestations of our flesh. These stem from deep-rooted false images through which we have unknowingly viewed life for years.

It is true that each of these manifestations of the flesh must be dealt with individually through repentance and cleansing by the blood of Jesus. However, stopping there and not going on to repent of the unconscious motivations behind them is similar to swatting flies in a kitchen with the door wide open while a full garbage pail sits exposed inside. You can swat flies very busily all day long, but if you never throw the garbage pail outside and close the door, there will always be more flies.

In other words, there are modes of operation based on certain false images from which superficial, nonvisible manifestations of our flesh arise. Sin operating in our flesh is a subtle, but very deadly, enemy resident within us illegally and bent on our destruction.

God's Word gives us a very clear picture of the operation of sin in our flesh through the prophet Amos. Sin is likened to a poisonous serpent, secretly residing in, and constantly poisoning the soul.

"It will be as though a man fled from a lion only to meet a bear, as though he entered his house and rested his hand on the wall, only to have a snake bite him" (Amos 5:19).

I can just picture a man being chased by a lion. He knows that if he is caught he will lose his life, and the lion will rip him to shreds. He runs and runs, and finally manages to lose the lion and escape. Just as he is catching his breath, he comes around a large rock and comes face to face with a huge bear. The bear rears on its hind legs and roars. You can image the despair of this poor fellow as he turns again and runs for his life.

Finally, he is able to elude the bear and escape. He decides that he has had enough adventure for one day, so he goes home to relax and unwind. You have to image a Middle Eastern home with a mortarless stone wall containing nooks and crannies between the stones. As the man sits down in his home to relax and leans up against the wall, a poisonous snake residing in the crevice suddenly strikes him on the hand, injecting its venomous poison.

Have you ever felt like this poor man? Everywhere you turn someone or something is there to oppose you, rob you, harm you, and destroy you. As I sought the Lord about this Scripture, He showed me that the lions and bears in our lives are people and circumstances putting destructive pressure on us. Lions or bears in your life could be bill collectors, the IRS, your boss, a fellow employee, unemployment, the economy, your wife, your husband, your kids, or your health. Any external problems that rob you of joy and peace are lions and bears. Sometimes it seems that as soon as you escape from one or have victory over it, another problem immediately arises to harass you.

Lions and bears are all problems that are visible and occupy your time and energy. The serpent, however, is hidden in the wall of your heart. It is not external, nor is it visible without revelation from God. It always seems to you, when lions and bears seek to destroy you, these problems are unrelated and external. They have come upon you due to circumstances beyond your control, or due to the sin of other people.

In many instances, however, this is not the truth. Very often, negative circumstances and relationships are due to sin in our flesh having deceived us and captured our souls. Sin in the flesh is the serpent hidden in the walls of our own hearts. The serpent is busy poisoning our minds, wills and emotions on the inside, which creates many of our external problems (lions and bears).

The primary problem is that because we've been deceived by the serpent in the wall, we don't see the connection between the external lions and bears and the internal operation of our own flesh. As long as the devil can keep our attention focused on fighting or fleeing from lions and bears, we will never see the poisonous snake hidden in the walls of our own hearts whose insidious venom deceives us and creates the situations that appear to be lions and bears.

If your life is riddled with lions and bears, you can be certain that this is not because God doesn't love you, is punishing you, or even that Satan is orchestrating all of these problems. It is simply due to a serpent, of which you have been unaware, hiding in your heart and poisoning your soul. Even if you are not aware of many lions and bears in your life, there is, nonetheless, a serpent operating subtly through you, bent on your destruction.

How is it that sin in our flesh is able to deceive us and take our souls captive? This happens primarily through the establishment in our souls of false images by which we measure and interpret all present and future words, experiences, and relationships. In Amos, chapter seven, the Word gives us more insight into this process:

"Thus He showed me, and behold, the Lord was standing by a vertical wall, with a plumb line in His hand. And the Lord said to me, 'What do you see, Amos?' And I said, 'A plumb line.' Then the Lord said, 'Behold, I am about to put a plumb line in the midst of My people Israel. I will spare them no longer'" (Amos 7:7-8).

In this Scripture, the Lord spoke to Amos about a plumb line. In ancient times a plumb line was used in the construction of a vertical structure, such as a wall, to ensure that the wall was not built crookedly. The plumb line was simply a metal weight hung on the end of a string, which, due to the gravitational pull of the earth, always hung perfectly vertical.

If a person in ancient times desired to build a wall out of bricks, he needed to hang a plumb line alongside the wall in order to ensure that it was being built exactly vertical and not leaning at some slight angle. This is not something that could be accurately sighted with the naked eye alone. If a man attempted to build a wall by merely sighting it with his natural eye, without the aid of a plumb line, his wall would surely be crooked to some slight degree and would lack the desired structural integrity. This is why a plumb line was always used.

The Lord told Amos that He would put a plumb line in the midst of His people. In other words, the Lord had a plumb line by which He wanted to measure the verticality of a wall in His people. What is the plumb line and what is the wall?

I believe that God's plumb line is His Word. We can measure whether our lives are straight by the Word, which is absolutely straight and never changes. The wall, I believe, is the soul of man, which is the seat of his personality. So the Lord was going to measure His peoples' souls, from which were manifested their thoughts, feelings, and actions, by His divine plumb line, His Word.

Your soul is similar to a vertical wall that has been built throughout your lifetime, one brick upon another. These building bricks are words and experiences that have formed images of yourself, God and others. Through the natural, logical interpretation of five-sense information, you establish, from a very young age, plumb line images by which you measure and view each new experience and set of words coming in. Thus, certain patterns of thought, emotion and behavior are established in your soul at a very early age according to the plumb line images of self, God and others by which you determine the truth about all experiences, words and relationships.

In order to build a vertical wall of structural integrity, one must use a plumb line. If someone tries to build a wall without the aid of a plumb line, the wall will undoubtedly be crooked and lack structural integrity. However, the worst situation of all is to build a wall using a perverted plumb line to which you believe and place all your trust and confidence as being a true vertical plumb line, but which, in fact, is not.

Suppose that you were building your wall with the aid of your plumb line. An enemy sneaks up very close to you and hides in the bushes with a powerful magnet. Each time you hold up your plumb line to check the verticality of your wall, the enemy raises his magnet and attracts the weight at the end of your line slightly off the vertical. As you continue to build your wall, believing that it is vertical because of your measurements, it, in fact, is deviating farther and farther off center.

This is exactly what has occurred in the life of every person on earth as he has progressed through life, building the wall of his personality according to the plumb lines of false images. The enemy is the devil. The magnet is sin in your flesh (and formerly in your spirit). The plumb lines are the images you have of yourself, God and others. As you progress through life as a Christian, your spirit is recreated and has the nature of Christ. But in many areas of your soul you still measure and draw conclusions about present experiences, words and relationships through perverted plumb line images in which you have trust and faith.

In most cases, because of the deceptiveness of sin in the flesh, Christians don't realize that many of their thoughts, emotions, and actions proceed from false plumb line images through which their flesh has captured their souls and operated for years. This establishment and operation of false images is the mechanism by which the venomous serpent of Amos 5 poisons the mind, will and emotions. The enemy, with his magnet, is not external to us, but the drawing off center of the plumb line is a process which occurs entirely within our souls (the wall). In a previous chapter, I shared about Steve who had judged his father for being lazy and ineffective. He judged others for being insensitive, and later reaped the fruit of those judgments. These judgments did not just spring up in Steve out of nowhere, but were merely bricks in an entire wall built through the use of a perverted plumb line image.

While Steve was growing up, it seemed to him that no matter how hard he tried he was never able to please his father. Due to his mind's interpretation of words and experiences, a plumb line image began to form, making him feel: "I'm a nobody in this world. No matter what I do and how hard I work, I'm never appreciated. Society in general and 'the system' are working against me to destroy me. But if I work hard enough, I'll finally be something, force change in society, and win appreciation and acceptance from those close to me."

After Steve was born again, he innocently viewed God through this same image and related to Him this way: "I'm unworthy to come to God, because I'm a nobody. It seems that no matter how hard I work, I'm never really pleasing to God. But if I work hard enough for the Lord, one day I'll be acknowledged and appreciated by others close to me, and by my Heavenly Father."

Unknown to Steve, his image became a plumb line by which he measured words, experiences, and relationships. He worked for Jesus, teaching, preaching and counseling for 12, 14, sometimes 18 hours a day. Nonetheless, he always felt unworthy before God and unappreciated by his family and others. Steve believed that his long work hours were proof of his diligent service to God, and this gave him satisfaction of accomplishment. He believed that the unworthiness was humility, and that any lack of appreciation from others was simply their lack of understanding of the importance of the ministry and his calling. Through all of this, Steve believed sincerely that he was walking in the spirit.

The truth was he was driven by his flesh to work long hours because he felt unworthy and unacceptable to God. Deep inside was a lie that told him, "If you are obedient and righteous enough, minister to enough people and excel in these things beyond others, you will win God's approval and acceptance." This false image of himself, and of God, was the mechanism by which the poisonous serpent in his flesh had deceived him, taken his soul captive, and was stunting his ministry, and destroying his family relationships.

Steve was already pleasing and acceptable to God; not on the basis of what he was doing, but on the basis of what the blood of Jesus Christ had already done. However, this false plumb line image kept Steve in bondage to his flesh. He was "trying to please God and earn appreciation," so the true nature of Jesus Christ in his spirit wasn't released to become manifest in his soul.

We see the mechanism of deception by sin in the flesh taking place here. Steve was certain that he was walking in the spirit. He considered himself to be committed, diligent, and even persecuted for Jesus' sake by his family and others who showed no appreciation or acceptance. In fact, he was being motivated by his flesh. He was not humble, but was actually in pride. He wasn't being persecuted for Jesus' sake. Rather, he was only reaping the consequences of the law of sin and death that had been sown by a destructive, venomous serpent hidden within him. Steve had no clue of the truth until the Holy Spirit revealed it to him. When he saw it, he repented, and his mind began being renewed to the truth of who he already was in the spirit. He began to be set free.

It is important to recognize that all of us have established false images through which our flesh controls and motivates us. We received these false images before we were born again and have continued to receive and reinforce many of them since we've known Jesus.

Perhaps you grew up in a Christian home and you don't believe that you are in any bondage to false images. I believe that, as we continue, the Holy Spirit will reveal to you bondages and modes of fleshly operation in your own life, of which you were unaware.

The world has one very powerful underlying message that initially perverts the plumb line within us. Every person on earth has, deep in their souls, received this message to one degree or another. The message proceeds from Satan, the god of this world, and is propagated throughout every area of life by the world system. This message is transmitted through government, education, employment, the media, family relationships, and even church. The ultimate message, simply stated, is that God does not love, honor, esteem, or accept you. Right along with this is the message that other people also do not love or accept you.

People in the world may say, "I don't believe in God, so I haven't received that message." But the Bible tells us that every person is born with an inherent knowledge of God (Romans 1:18-21), and I believe that it is the receipt of this false message that has primarily turned people away from God. Non-Christians may only admit to sensing the rejection of other people. But deep inside there is ultimately a doubt or denial of God's love as well. This doubt of God's love results immediately in fear rising up in a man's soul. As you recall from chapter three, fear operates the law of sin and death in one's life. Fear prevents one from receiving God's love, trusting in Him in faith, and thereby walking in the law of the spirit of life in Christ Jesus.

What is the nature of fear that results from the doubt of God's love for us? What is it a fear of? The author of Hebrews tells us that it is ultimately a fear of death.

*"Since then the children share in flesh and blood, He Himself likewise also partook of the same, that through death He might render powerless him who had the power of death, that is, the devil; and might deliver those who through **fear of death** were subject to slavery all their lives" (Hebrews 2:14-15).*

Fear of death keeps us in slavery and bondage to our flesh and, ultimately, to the devil. What is death? Death is the absence of life. There is ultimately a fear deep inside each person of the termination of physical life. However, there is also an equally strong fear of soulish death. What I mean by soulish death is the loss of life in a particular area of our minds, wills or emotions.

Our own flesh, motivated by fear, always seeks its own preservation and survival. This is true, whether it be physical survival, mental survival, or emotional survival. The fear of losing life or not surviving in any of these areas is the fear of death that Hebrews 2:15 says has "kept us in slavery all our lives."

Fear of not having an emotional need met is fear of death. We are afraid that we will be robbed of life, emotionally. When a husband is afraid of the fleshly reaction of his wife because he is two hours late for dinner, he is afraid of receiving words and emotions that will destroy his emotional well-being and bring death into his soul. When a child is afraid of punishment by his father, he fears emotional death. When an intellectual considers yielding his mind to Jesus Christ, he fears mental death. He is afraid that his mental well-being may be threatened. When a child is told by a teacher that he is stupid and will never succeed, he fears death in his personal identity. He is afraid of being a worthless failure.

No person can survive emotionally or even physically with his soul being full of death.

If death enters a person's soul, he will be motivated by fear of that death to do whatever his carnal mind deems necessary to extricate himself from that death. Fear, of course, will motivate him to do so in the flesh.

Therefore, fear is the most powerful, often

Therefore, fear is the most powerful, often unconscious, motivating force through which the serpent in our hearts can poison our souls.Jesus said in John 10:10 that He came to bring us abundant life. The Greek word for this life which Jesus brings is *zoe*. *Zoe* life is the eternal life of God which God originally breathed into Adam's spirit and soul in Genesis 2:7, the life of God that comes into our spirits and recreates them when we are born again. *Zoe* life is the life that the Father has in Himself and gave to the Son (John 5:26). This is the life that John said was in Jesus and was the light of men (John 1:4).

Zoe life is the supernatural life of God, resident in our born-again spirits, constantly recharged in our spirits as we dwell in the Word and prayer. *Zoe* life can only enter the soul through a born-again spirit. When your spirit has preeminence in your soul, you walk in the law of the spirit of life *(zoe)* in Jesus, and your soul becomes full of *zoe* life. However, when you walk in the flesh, you cut off your soul from the *zoe* life of God in your spirit.

Another Greek word in the New Testament sometimes translated as life is the word *psuche*. *Psuche* literally means "soul" and is the word from which we derive such words in English as psyche, or psychology (the study of *psuche)*. Where *psuche* is translated "life" in the Bible, you can usually substitute the word "soul," which refers to soul-life. Jesus told us in Mark's gospel:

> *"For whoever wishes to save his life (psuche) shall lose it; but whoever loses his life (psuche) for My sake and the gospel's sake shall save it. For what does it profit a man to gain the whole world, and forfeit his soul? For what shall a man give in exchange for his soul?" (Mark 9:35-37).*

We see in this passage that the word translated "life" is actually the Greek word *psuche,* meaning "soul." So Jesus said that whoever seeks to save his own soul will lose it, and whoever relinquishes his soul to Jesus will save it. Jesus is not speaking here about spiritual life, salvation. Neither does He refer to physical life, but He is talking about *psuche*, the soul life.

What could cause a man to seek to save his own soul life from perishing? Fear of soulish death. If your flesh is ruling your soul in a certain area and you, the spirit man, desire to crucify that area of flesh and yield to your spirit, what will occur in your soul? Your flesh, of course, will fight for survival. It will attempt to motivate you through fear of death to not terminate its life. Your flesh will tell you that it is giving you life and peace; if you cut it off, you will experience soulish death. The truth is, your flesh prevents you from experiencing true life, the *zoe* life of God in your soul.

Let's take a blatant example of a woman in bondage to alcohol. She is in slavery due to fear of death. She derives a measure of peace and comfort in her soul through the alcohol. If she considers crucifying her flesh, walking in the spirit, and trusting God to bring peace and comfort to her soul, a terrible fear rises up immediately within her. Her flesh tells her that she will perish emotionally. If she doesn't drink, she will feel down, depressed and so full of lack of peace and discomfort that she won't be able to stand it. This is the poisonous deception of the serpent in the heart. Her flesh tells her that she will perish if she mortifies her flesh and walks in the spirit. Of course, the truth is just the opposite. If she mortifies the flesh and walks in the spirit, the *zoe* life of God comes flooding into her soul and brings life, peace, comfort, joy, and love.

When your flesh motivates you, through fear, to seek preservation from death in an area of your soul life, you will walk in the flesh, thereby cutting yourself off from the *zoe* life of God in your spirit. In the end, you will lose the very life you attempt to obtain:

"It is the Spirit who gives life; the flesh profits nothing, the **words that I have spoken to you are spirit and are life"** *(John 6:63).*

Look at three Scriptures describing this, all together:

"For whoever wishes to save his life shall lose it; but whoever loses his life for My sake and the gospel's shall save it"

(Mark 8:35). "And might deliver those who through fear of death were subject to slavery all their lives" (Hebrews 2:15). "Walk in the futility of their mind, being darkened in their understanding, excluded from the life of God, because of the ignorance that is in them, because of the hardness of their heart" (Ephesians 4:17-18).

If you seek to save your own *psuche* (soul), you will be motivated by fear of death, and will walk in the futility of your mind (flesh). You will be excluded from the *zoe* (life) of God, and will, as a result, lose your *psuche* (soul). Our souls are only saved when by walking in the spirit (Romans 8:13) we put to death their fleshly control, receive humbly an implanting of God's Word in our souls (James 1:21), and receive His love.

As I mentioned earlier, doubting God's love gives rise to a fear of death. Some Christians are motivated by fear of physical death, and others by spiritual death (loss of salvation). These, however, are usually conscious motivations of which the person is aware. Every Christian, unless he walks 100 percent of the time in the spirit, is also motivated by fear of soulish death. This fear is often an unconscious motivating factor and can motivate unsuspecting Christians not to walk in faith.

Fear of death in the soul manifests itself primarily in two areas, both of which are rooted in the doubt of God's love. The first of these is in the realm of our personal identities.

In order not to experience tremendous emotional death, a person must feel of value and importance. However, when a person receives the message that God doesn't love him, that person's self-worth is jeopardized. He thinks to himself, "If God doesn't love, honor, or esteem me, then I am of very little value. I am unimportant. Other people are of more value and importance than I am. I am a nobody!"

Value is determined by love, honor, and esteem. Those things which you love and honor, in which you invest large amounts of money and time in acquiring, have great value to you. Other people whom you love and esteem are very valuable to you. Ultimate value in the universe is determined by God's love and honor. That which God loves is valuable. That which God does not love or honor has little value. The Bible tells us that God has a very great love for every person, and therefore every person is ultimately of very great value (John 3:16). This is the truth and basis of God's divine plumb line by which we are meant to measure all words, experiences, and relationships.

The second manifestation of fear of death is in the realm of personal welfare. If a man believes that his needs will not be met, and he will not be cared for or benefited by God, he will be motivated by great fear. He will think to himself, "Because God doesn't love me, He isn't really concerned about me. He doesn't have my best interests at heart, and isn't faithful or trustworthy to meet my needs, protect me, and care for me. I would be a fool to entrust my very life to someone who is more powerful than I, whom I am not certain loves me or has my welfare and best interest at heart."

These two manifestations of fear of death are an almost instantaneous reaction to the doubt of God's love. Whenever God's love for you is in question, your personal identity and your welfare, both of which are rooted in Him, are suddenly jeopardized. Fear, then, is manifest immediately in both these areas. When you doubt God's love, you cannot trust Him. If your trust and faith are not in God, you must place them in someone or something else — usually yourself! This will always produce fear, because God is the only one who can be 100 percent trustworthy and faithful to you.

If your trust is in yourself, or anyone else, you will be in fear because neither you nor they have either the wisdom or the ability to always act in your best interest, for your welfare. Only God can do so. Doubt of God's love always results in fear of death regarding personal value and welfare which is the primary motivating force of the flesh. Only receipt of God's love can vanquish the torment of fear of death:

"There is no fear in love; but perfect love casteth out fear; because fear hath torment. He that feareth is not made perfect in love" (I John 4:18, King James Version).

Through creating doubt of God's love, and the resulting fear, the serpent beguiled Adam and Eve. In Genesis 3:1, the serpent questioned God's Word to Eve: "Indeed, has God said..." The serpent began by sowing a seed of doubt in God's Word. In verses 4 and 5, he said, "You surely shall not die! For God knows that in the day you eat from it, your eyes will be opened, and you will be like God, knowing good and evil."

I believe the serpent may have given Eve a little pitch something like the following: "God doesn't really love you. You are of no value in your present state. You could become of great value, however, if you took some steps to get out from under your slavery to God. If you were to eat of the fruit, you would become like God and be just as wise and powerful as He is. You wouldn't have to be dependent upon Him anymore. God knows all of this and is very threatened by your potential. He is afraid of losing His own status and authority. In fact," the serpent continues, "God's only means of protection is to deceive and keep you in ignorance.

He may have told you not to eat of this fruit, but He said it for His own welfare. God is not acting in your best interest, but in His own. He is selfish. He is intimidated by you. And He has duped you into not fulfilling your real potential. These guidelines are not according to your best interest. Come on, Eve. Wake up! You have put your confidence in someone who has lied to you in order to keep you in bondage to Him so He can retain his power. Eat of the fruit and become like God."

With these words in verses 4 and 5, the serpent caused Eve to (1) doubt God's love for her; (2) question her value as a person, and; (3) doubt God's concern for her and His faithfulness to meet her needs and act in her best interest.

I am certain that a terrible sinking feeling took place

in Eve's heart as she began to believe, through the serpent's beguiling, that the very one to whom she had entrusted her heart and life had betrayed her and lied to her for His own selfish reasons. The next logical step in her thinking probably was, "If God is a deceiver and isn't really concerned for my welfare, I had better look after myself in order to survive physically and emotionally. I thought that I was precious and a valuable person. But now I see that I am nothing but a worthless fool. Well, I am going to become somebody and do important, worthwhile things. I am going to eat of that fruit and become just as wise, powerful and important as God."

Eve then ate of the fruit in an attempt to exalt herself in pride to be equal with God and meet her own needs. This beguiling and poisoning of the soul was the mechanism by which the serpent established in Eve a false plumb line by which she measured God's Word and her relationship to Him. The serpent's basic message is that God doesn't love you. The two manifestations of fear that accompany it, fear of no value, and fear of not having needs met, are the magnetic power that draws the plumb line off center, creating a perverted, non-vertical plumb line, through which life is then viewed and the personality developed. Every person on earth has been bombarded continually with this message and has received it along with the accompanying fear to varying degrees. Some people are consciously aware of being motivated by fear, because they often feel worthless and unimportant and are afraid that their needs won't be met. Others may not consciously be aware of this, but their souls are motivated by fear without their knowledge.

Although various people react in different ways to their doubt of God's love and the accompanying fears, this message is the common underlying, motivating power of the flesh in everyone. Let's examine in greater detail the fear of death regarding our personal identity.

If you were to ask some people, "Do you feel as though your work and activities are unimportant and meaningless?" or "Do you feel unimportant and unworthy of esteem?" many would respond affirmatively. I have found this to be particularly true of wives of pastors or "important" spiritual, business, or political leaders. Such wives often view their husbands as being very important, but view themselves as valueless. This is by no means limited to women, however.

Many people who are very "successful" spiritually, or in business or politics do not experience conscious worthlessness. In fact, they appear to others as confident. However, unless such people have truly gained the knowledge of who they are in the spirit, there will be a false plumb line image regarding their identities.

It was very difficult for me to see this false plumb line in my life. I have been a person who was not consciously aware of doubt of God's love for me. If someone had told me that I was motivated by a fear of inadequacy, worthlessness, and unimportance, I would have rejected that counsel and thought, "You are way off base." Ever since I was born again, I felt very confident in my identity in Jesus Christ. I had always perceived myself as being very self-confident, and not in bondage to low self-esteem or worthlessness.

However, the Lord began to reveal to me in the spirit that my flesh had deceived me. My soul was motivated by the fear of not being valued and esteemed. The Lord revealed this to me in the following way.

I had wanted to share a particular vision for ministry that the Lord had given me with Wallace and Marilyn Hickey, the pastors of our church. I had shared this vision with Christy James, director of the counseling center, and she agreed that I should share it with the Hickeys. One Sunday during an open house in the new ministry building, I happened to see Marilyn in her office, approached her and mentioned that my wife and I had something we'd like to share with Wally and her. I asked if we could meet, and she responded, "That would be fine. We also have something to share with you."

The next day, when I saw Christy, I wanted to report to her about the conversation with Marilyn. I told her with excitement, "Christy, I saw Marilyn last night, and, praise the Lord, before I could even approach her, she told me that she and Wally had something on their hearts to share with Jan and me. She wanted to arrange to have lunch with us sometime soon."

Just after I finished speaking, the Holy Spirit spoke into my spirit, "You liar. That is not the way it happened. Repent, and confess to Christy the truth." I thought to myself, "Well, I guess that wasn't exactly true, but who cares? Christy isn't going to hire a private detective to find out how the conversation really went. It is immaterial. The main point is that we are going to meet with Wally and Marilyn and share this ministry vision. It doesn't really matter exactly who invited whom."

The Holy Spirit said, "I care. It *does* matter, because that is a lie. It is sin, and you don't hate it. As a matter of fact, you don't even acknowledge it as sin, and that deeply grieves Me." He went on to say, "This isn't the first time you have lied like this, but your heart is so hardened that you haven't seen it before. Now that you see it, you don't even think it is bad. But it is bad. It is sin operating through your flesh, and it is bringing death. When you don't repent and you let it continue, you are in the flesh, and you are hating Me."

As the Lord spoke into my spirit, I felt convicted. Godly sorrow fell upon me. I felt terrible that I had hated God and that I had continued to allow my flesh to capture my soul. I repented and asked the Lord's forgiveness. Then I went back to Christy, confessed the lie to her, and asked for her forgiveness also.

I asked the Lord, "Where did that lie come from? I didn't plan it in advance. I didn't consciously design this lie to tell Christy. It just came out of my mouth before I even thought about it. Lord, where did it come from?"

God showed me, "Your lie was rooted in pride." Pride is the desire to exalt oneself above others and above the truth." He also said, "You were in pride; you wanted to exalt yourself in order to make Christy think that you are so important that Wally and Marilyn are constantly seeking you out to consult with you and share their plans. You wanted her to highly esteem and honor you. Therefore, your flesh decided to twist the truth to generate that honor and esteem from Christy."

I said, "Yes, Lord. But why did I allow pride to capture my mind and will?"

He then responded, "It was due to the fear of not being accepted and esteemed by Christy. Your trust and confidence was not in Me and in My nature in your spirit. What you have always perceived as self-confidence and self-esteem is just that — confidence in *your self*, esteem for *your own* intelligence, creativity, and ability in *your own flesh*. You have said your trust and confidence is in who you are in Christ. But in most areas of life, your trust and confidence is in *you*, and in *your* ability to be obedient to me, *your* ability to minister My Word to others, and *your* ability to conduct relationships with others."

Because my confidence was in myself, I feared that appearing unimportant, unrighteous, or unproductive would cause a lack of acceptance and esteem. My fear of these things came for one reason: Because that was the way that I really felt about myself. "If you were truly confident and trusting in the truth of who you are in Christ in the spirit, you would have no need to operate in pride, twist the truth, or lie to others. Deep inside, you don't really believe that I love and esteem you, either. You are not resting in My love for you."

After the Lord revealed this to me, I repented not only of lying, but also of pride, fear, unbelief, and my false self-image of having little value. This entire false plumb line image had operated through my flesh, unconsciously, all my life. Yet I had never seen it until the Lord revealed it through this experience.

In the past, I had used "positive or negative self-image," "self-esteem," and "self-acceptance" to describe how Christians perceived themselves. However, the Lord showed me these are terms imported from the world and plugged into a Christian context. But they are not biblical. They conjure up in the mind a view of ourselves according to the world's model of man, and not according to God's model. According to the Word, our self-images are resident in our souls but can emanate either from our flesh or our spirits. Any image we have of ourself that proceeds from our born-again, recreated spirits is correct. Any other image is a wrong, false self-image that is not according to God's truth about us.

During all the years that I was born again, I considered myself to have a good self-image and a high degree of self-confidence. On the other hand, I thought that Jan, my wife, had a poor self-image and little self-confidence. The world and the church viewed me as more successful and more productive for God than Jan was, and I thought so too. She was depressed more often and seemed to have more problems than I did.

I thought, "If she could just trust in the Lord more, and come to a better self image, her problems would go away. She would be successful, like me." I thought that I was trusting in God and that Jan was not.

Eventually, the Lord showed me how deceptive that type of thinking is. Neither of our self images were better or "more spiritual" than the other. Jan's self image and also mine emanated from the same place — the flesh. I was perceived as being in victory, and Jan was perceived as being in defeat, but, in fact, we were both being governed by our flesh. One self image wasn't good and the other poor. Both were simply false. I can only share this testimony now because both Jan and I have repented of these false images and are experiencing greater and greater freedom as the Holy Spirit renews our minds to the truth of who we really are in the spirit.

No matter how "good" your self image is, if it is rooted in trust and confidence in yourself and your abilities, it is rooted in your flesh and it has the same degree of "goodness" as all your "righteous deeds" that might also proceed from your flesh:

"For all of us have become like one who is unclean, and all

*our righteous deeds are like a filthy garment; and all of us wither
like a leaf, and our iniquities, like the wind, take us away" (Isaiah
64:6).*

Jesus said, in John 3:6, "That which is born of
flesh is flesh, and that which is born of spirit is spirit."
This includes your self image or soulish experience of
yourself. The concept of good or poor self image, self
esteem, self confidence, or self acceptance is a wordly
concept that is inconsistent with God's Word. The Lord
told me, "Stop using that concept and allow Me to renew
your mind to the truth. You are a recreated spirit being
whose primary need is to have your mind, will, and
emotions renewed to the truth of that recreation (2
Corinthians 5:17). Any image of yourself rooted in your
flesh is neither good nor poor; it is just wrong. No
matter how "good" it appears, it has been constructed
according to a perverted plumb line. It is of the flesh and
can only reproduce after its own kind and yield the fruit
of the flesh (Galatians 5:19-21). Any image of ourselves
rooted in our born-again spirits is correct. It also can
only reproduce after its own kind and will only yield in
life the fruit of the spirit (Galatians 5:22-23).

As we continue to examine the false image, we find
that our reactions in the flesh differ, depending upon
whether we consciously experience the reality of fear.

If one consciously experiences himself as having
little value and importance, the false image through
which he views God, himself, and others will be different than that of one who consciously experiences himself
as valuable, esteemed and important. It is this fear which
motivates people to walk in the flesh.

Please keep in mind that we are only now
discussing the false plumb lines of our flesh. We are
discussing the way in which sin in our flesh has
deceived us and captured our souls. When you recognize
some of the following thinking and behavior in yourself,
remember that we are not describing the truth in the spirit
about you, but the lie in your flesh. Therefore, don't

identify yourself or anyone else according to these false plumb line images. But if you recognize these images in yourself, repent, and ask the Holy Spirit to begin to renew your mind to the truth in your spirit.

The conscious experience of the message, "I am of no value because God doesn't love me" determines primarily whether you perceive yourself to be a somebody or a nobody. If you consciously experience yourself as worthless, you will perceive yourself to be unimportant, having nothing of value to contribute to the Kingdom or society. On the other hand, if you are not aware of consciously feeling worthless, you will experience yourself to be an important person with a valuable contribution to make to the Kingdom and society.

The conscious experience of value determines the basic plumb line image of yourself, God, and others. The Christian who experiences conscious-worthlessness feels that he is not really loved, valued or esteemed by God or others. He feels that he is never appreciated. He also expects that others will not acknowledge him or treat him with respect. Because of the law of sowing and reaping in judgment or expectancy, he often has experiences that confirm to him the "truth" of this self-image.

The Christian who does not consciously experience the fear of having no value, feels that he is worthy of God's love and esteem. Consciously, he may say this is because of his trust in Jesus, but inside he believes it is because of his commitment, obedience to God, and his righteousness. He expects others to acknowledge him and treat him with respect because of his standing in the Kingdom and in society.

Both of these images are false self-images, because they are born of the flesh and not of the spirit. However, the world calls the first a poor self-image and the second a good self-image. The person with the second appears to be more successful than the first, but the truth is that sin and death reign through both.

Let's now examine the second manifestation of fear of death. This is the fear regarding one's personal welfare. It is the fear of not being taken care of, or of having one's needs met. Like the first manifestation of fear, this fear can be experienced consciously by some, while it motivates others without their conscious-awareness.

Once again, before the Lord opened up to me how this fear was unconsciously motivating me, I had no idea of its operation through my flesh. On the same day in which the Lord had convicted me of lying to Christy and of the fear of not being esteemed and valued, He began to reveal to me, also, the unconscious operation in me of the fear of death regarding my emotional welfare.

I had scheduled counseling appointments all day until 8 p.m. and told Jan that I would be home by 8:30 p.m., after my last appointment. However, my last appointment finished late. As I left my office, I ran into one of the other counselors who began to share something from the Word that God has shown her. As we talked, we both continued to receive new insight from the Word on this particular topic.

I left the church at 9:45 p.m. to drive home. As I drove, my spirit was full of excitement over the new revelation and insight I'd just received. I was singing and praising God while I was driving. Suddenly, I became aware that while my mouth was busy singing praises to God, my mind was busy thinking about what I would tell Jan when I arrived home. I found myself thinking, "Jan's going to be angry because I'm an hour and a half late. She will ask me why I am late, and I don't want to tell her that it's because I was talking with another woman about spiritual things. She will be angry because I was spending my limited time with another woman instead of her. She will also be angry because I was preferring ministry and my own pleasure above my family. It would be better to tell her that my last appointment ran late (which was slightly true — 10 minutes). That way she won't be quite so angry."

My spirit spoke into my mind, "Why don't you just tell her the truth?" My mind answered, "She will be really angry, and it will be unpleasant for me. I don't want to have to bear that unpleasantness and accusation. I'd rather modify the story to mitigate the consequences."

The Holy Spirit spoke to me in the spirit, "You're making up a lie again. You're not merely modifying unimportant details. You are making up a lie to tell your wife because you're afraid of the consequences of telling the truth. You're not trusting me to meet your needs emotionally and to work in Jan."

It was then that I began to recognize the fear. I had almost decided that I'd rather tell the lie and avoid as much of Jan's anger as possible than tell the truth and face Jan's potential anger. I thought I could repent later. At this point, I saw how much fear I had regarding my wife and her potential emotional reaction to me. Fear in me was very powerfully motivating me to choose lying over truthfulness, and sin over righteousness. Each time I began to consider telling the truth, I felt the fear, emotionally, as my mind considered the potential consequences with Jan. I was experiencing the fear of death in my emotions. Therefore, I had decided to take steps that would meet my own emotional needs by lying, rather than face the prospect of mental and emotional torment and death (Hebrews 2:15).

As I experienced fear of death and, for the first time, recognized it consciously, God told me, "I have not given you a spirit of fear." This fear emanated not from my spirit, but from my flesh. Upon recognizing this, I repented and let my spirit begin to reign in my mind and emotions.

Basically, the fear of having my needs unmet had deceived me, captured my soul, and caused me to view Jan in the flesh, not in the spirit. Thus, I had held her in bondage through a false expectation based on past experience. God told me to repent of viewing my wife through the fleshly expectations. I repented of dishonoring my time commitment to Jan and asked her forgiveness when I got home. Jan forgave me and reacted to me in the spirit, and the entire negative consequence that I had expected was short circuited and never came to pass.

I did not experience emotional torment or death, but instead I experienced the *zoe* life of God.

Like the first fear regarding personal identity, the fear of not having one's needs met manifests itself differently, depending upon the conscious awareness of that fear. Conscious present experience of having one's needs met or unmet determines the awareness of fear of not having one's needs met in the future. Conscious awareness of this fear determines whether one has hope of success and victory in life, or whether one expects failure and defeat — whether he'll be a winner or a loser.

The Christian who consciously experiences the reality of fear regarding his personal welfare (that because God doesn't love the person, his needs won't be met) will feel that there is little or no hope of success and victory in life for him. Because he usually experiences his needs as being unmet, he fears that they won't be met in the future either, because God "hasn't helped in the past." Such a person thinks odds against winning God's favor for help are too great, so he might as well give up.

The Christian who does not consciously experience the reality of this fear, on the other hand, expects victory and success in life. Because he experiences his needs as being met, he feels that he has already won God's favor and blessing, or at least that the odds of doing so are very good. He believes that he will overcome the devil, negative circumstances, and other people who try to stand against him, and, therefore, will ultimately experience victory and success. He believes that this is due to his trust in Jesus and his authority as a believer. But, in reality, he is actually trusting his own ability to hear God, be obedient to Him, and be righteous in order to retain God's favor and blessing.

Once again, both of these images are false, because they are born of flesh, not the spirit. The world calls the first person a "loser" and the second a "winner." The truth is, once again, that sin and death reign through the flesh, equally, in both cases.

Many times, because our minds are unrenewed in

this area, we try to motivate people through preaching, teaching and counseling, to repent of a "poor" self-image and come into a "good" self-image, or to lay aside self-images of failure and defeat and become motivated toward success and victory. Frequently, all we do is get people to "repent" from one mode of walking in the flesh to another. The problem is, they never come into the knowledge of the truth of who they are in the spirit.

We have now identified four different modes of walking in the flesh based on four different plumb line images. These are predicated upon the conscious experience of the fear of death regarding our personal identity and welfare. We can have a Christian who feels like: (1) a nobody, but has hope of victory; (2) a somebody, and has hope of victory; (3) a nobody, with no hope of victory; (4) a somebody, with no hope of victory.

The following chart represents these four modes of walking in the flesh in relationship to the conscious experience of the message of both manifestations of fear.

Experience of Fear		**Plumb Line Self Image Experience Self As A:**
Identity No Value	*Welfare Needs Not Met*	
1. *Conscious*	*Unconscious*	Nobody, hope-victory-winner
2. *Unconscious*	*Unconscious*	Somebody, hope-victory-winner
3. *Conscious*	*Conscious*	Nobody, no hope-defeat-loser
4. *Unconscious*	*Conscious*	Somebody, no hope-defeat-loser

Our flesh entertains two primary reactions in order to deal with the two manifestations of the fear of death. These reactions are pride and rebellion. Pride reacts due to fear of being worthless, while rebellion reacts due to the fear of not having one's needs met. You may recall these reactions to fear in Adam and Eve in the Garden.

Pride focuses on, and trusts in, oneself instead of in God. It is the exaltation of self through distrust of God, whether in arrogance or self-pity. Essentially, pride is our flesh's way of coping with the self-image and feeling of having little value and importance. When the message comes to you, "You are no good and of no value, you are unimportant," your flesh responds immediately in pride, taking your attention off of Jesus Christ and placing it on yourself. This will manifest in two different ways, depending on the conscious experience of the fear of having little value.

If you consciously experience the fear of being valueless to God, your flesh will motivate you in attempts to earn God's love and esteem (obey God, be righteous, etc.). But you are trusting in yourself and you become convinced that it is impossible to win God's esteem and honor. Pride motivates self-pity. This is the same pride as before, but it focuses inward in defeat.

On the other hand, if you don't consciously experience the fear of having no value, pride will motivate your flesh to believe that you are already worthy of God's love. Why? Because of your past and current righteousness and obedience to Him. Pride motivates you to look to your own works and trust in yourself. In both cases, pride causes one to trust in oneself and one's flesh.

The second manifestation of fear of death, that of having one's needs unmet, begins to motivate the soul whenever God's love for us is in question. The fleshly reaction to this fear is rebellion, opposition to or fleeing from a relationship. If you are in relationship with, and under the authority of, a particular person whom you don't trust and don't believe has your welfare and benefit in mind, your flesh—motivated by self-preservation and fear of death—will not be interested in submitting any part of your life to that person. You will relate to that person out of fear, and your only natural choice will be to either oppose and undermine the authority of that person, or flee and terminate the relationship. This is rebellion.

When we doubt God's love for us and are afraid that He won't meet our needs, then we won't trust Him with our lives. We also won't trust Him in others whom He has placed in authority over us. Thus, we rebel against God and other people. This is what I was doing when I dreamed up a little lie to tell Jan about why I was late. Rebellion takes the form of either direct opposition to a person feared, or fleeing from them. In either opposing or fleeing, the rebellion can take the form of open, blatant rebellion or the covert, insidious, undermining of authority.

We have all seen both of these types of rebellion in children. Some children openly tell their parents, "No, go jump in the lake!" Others say, "Yes," but then find sneaky ways not to comply and thereby undermine their parents' intentions.

Rebellion can manifest itself in at least four ways: (1) Open opposition; (2) open flight; (3) hidden opposition; and (4) hidden flight.

Here is an example. A student, when asked to sit down in a classroom, can either (1) remain standing and say, "No"; (2) turn and walk out of the classroom; (3) sit down, but remain standing in his attitude, and find "legitimate" excuses to stand up; or (4) sit down, withdraw into self-pity, and refuse to relate to the teacher anymore.

It is not important to know what factors, besides fear, determine these manifestations of rebellion. It is only necessary to understand that all of these manifestations are rebellion and are rooted in fear and doubt of God's love. They must be recognized and repented of.

All forms of pride and rebellion emanate from sin in our flesh, operate through perverted plumb line images of God, self and others based on doubt of God's love and the accompanying fear, and motivate us without our conscious-awareness. This is the serpent in the wall of our souls beguiling and capturing us through false plumb line images already deeply established there.

The intensity of pride and rebellion operating in us

is directly proportional to the intensity of the fear to which they are linked, and is represented by the distance that the plumb line is drawn off center. As the fear of having no value or importance becomes stronger, pride becomes a stronger force in the flesh to compensate for the increased feeling of worthlessness. As the fear of not having one's needs met becomes stronger, rebellion becomes a stronger force in the flesh to compensate for the increased fear of harm. The more that fear intensifies, due to a circumstance or experience, the more likely it is that a person may attempt to change modes of walking in the flesh as the fear moves from unconscious motivation into his conscious-awareness.

No single mode of walking in the flesh will exactly describe any one person. Since the plumb line can be positioned anywhere between totally vertical and totally horizontal, depending upon the intensity of fear, there are an almost indefinite number of modes of walking in the flesh. In the following chapters, I will describe four modes which we can think of as the four boundary modes with many progressive shades between.

It is also possible for a person to walk in the spirit in part of his life and in the flesh in another part. He may, at one time, walk in the flesh in a particular mode in some particular area of life; and, at another time, walk in the spirit. People can change modes, walk in different modes in different areas of life, or can flip-flop between modes in one particular area of life.

It is unlikely that any Christian walks 100 percent of the time in all areas of his life in the flesh exactly according to one of the four modes that I will describe. This is not the critical point. I am not attempting to create a new doctrine or theory into which all Christians walking in flesh should fit. Nobody will fit these descriptions exactly. However, as you read, you should ask the Lord to reveal to you, in the spirit, the pertinent characteristics of the mode in which your own flesh has deceived you, taken captive your soul, and has been operating through you without your awareness. Once you have received revelation of a mode of flesh in which you've been walking, don't continue to identify yourself that way. But repent and identify yourself in the spirit.

The various characteristics of these modes of operation in the flesh are not "negative personality traits", "weakness in our character", or "personal problems." Thinking in this way causes us to identify with our own flesh, believe that characteristic is *me*, and then try to stop or overcome it. This will always lead to an attempt to overcome our flesh using the Word as a law in our mind. In Romans 7, however, Paul said clearly that this is not you. Don't identify personally with sin in your flesh. It is sin operating through you, but it is not *you*.

Let's briefly recount the basic self-image of each of the four modes of fleshly operation. In the first mode, the person operates on the basis of believing, "I'm unimportant, not loved, and a nobody. But I can ultimately become a somebody and have victory in my life through what I do."

The person operating in the second mode believes, "I'm important and valuable. I'm a somebody because of who I am and what I do. I can remain a somebody by continuing what I'm doing now, and by doing even greater things in the future. I will have victory in my life."

The person operating in the third mode believes, "I'm unimportant, a nobody. I can't win in life. I'm doomed to this terrible life, and I'll always be a nobody. I won't have victory. There's no point in trying."

The person operating in the fourth mode believes, "I'm a somebody and am important and of value. However, I don't have victory now and won't because others (perhaps God) are against me and I can't win. It's unfair, and I'm doomed to this life of defeat."

Health, financial, relational, occupational and other such circumstances are not only determined by, but also help determine the modes of flesh in which Christians may walk.

These circumstances are all tied primarily to the fear of death. Consequently, people whose circumstances are positive are usually found operating in the first and second mode. People whose circumstances are not so good usually walk in the third or fourth mode.

Every one of the ways in which we can walk in the flesh is rooted in the lie that God's love, esteem, favor and blessing come on the basis of performance. "If I perform adequately, God will love me and bless me." Each of these modes motivates a believer to unwittingly trust in "works righteousness."

This can be so subtle it motivates Christians to judge others who overtly walk in "works righteousness."

When I lied to Christy about my conversation with Marilyn, I didn't choose to do so; my flesh captured my soul and began to "play the tape," or operate in the groove that had been established in that area of my soul.

Once our flesh begins to operate in a particular groove, we have little choice over our thoughts and behavior. Then, flesh plays that which has been prerecorded on the tape. It has already captured the mind, emotions, and will, in deception. We aren't really aware that our flesh is controlling us. However, when we become aware of it by revelation from the Holy Spirit, we can repent and allow the Word and the blood of Jesus to supernaturally fill in that groove. He will cut a brand new groove according to the truth of Christ in the spirit.

Many Christians believe that hardness of heart only comes through willful disobedience. This is not true, however, and this belief makes it difficult for us to recognize hardness of heart, because we are not aware of any willful disobedience to God. But each time we operate in the flesh, even when it is unknown to us because sin has deceived us, we are hardening our hearts:

"Now this I affirm and testify in the Lord, that you must no longer live as the Gentiles do, in the futility of their minds; they are darkened in their understanding, alienated from the life of God because of the ignorance that is in them, due to their hardness of heart" (Ephesians 4:17-18).

Hardness of heart comes anytime that we accept a lie for the truth, believe we're in the spirit when we're in the flesh, or believe something about God or ourselves that is not according to the truth, whether it comes through conscious rebellion or unwittingly through deception. The result is the same in either case. Our hearts are hardened in those areas, we are cut off from the life of God, and we experience the consequences of the law of sin and death.

The grooves in the soul are areas of hardness of heart. When a false image is created, it forms a pattern of thinking, feeling, and behaving (groove) that is molded and hardened by each new word or experience viewed through that false image. Sin in our flesh is very deceptive, and much hardness of heart comes unknowingly through the deceitfulness of sin in our flesh.

"But exhort one another every day, as long as it is called 'today', that none of you may be hardened by the deceitfulness of sin" (Hebrews 3:13).

Mark 6 records the incident of Jesus walking on the water out to the boat in which the disciples were riding one night. The disciples were initially frightened, but then they recognized Jesus.

"And He went up into the boat with them and the wind ceased, (sank to rest as if exhausted by its own beating). And they were astonished exceedingly — beyond measure. For they failed to consider or understand (the teaching and meaning of the miracle of) the loaves; (in fact) their hearts had grown callous — had become dull and had lost the power of understanding" (Mark 6:51-52, Amplified Bible).

Because the disciples viewed their experience with Jesus through false plumb line images, they didn't relate to Jesus according to the truth of who He was and what He was doing. Consequently, rather than being transformed through their experience with Jesus, their hearts were merely hardened and they weren't set free.

The degree of hardness of heart in any particular

area is directly proportional to the degree of faith and confidence placed in the lie. Our minds have been conformed to the world in many areas through the deceitfulness of sin and our hearts hardened in those areas. Our souls are in desperate need of cleansing and purging, and our minds need to be renewed. This process of transformation by the renewing of the mind is mentioned by Paul in Romans 12:2.

Many Christians are tremendously frustrated in their lives with the Lord "because of the ignorance that is in them, because of the hardness of their hearts." They have often done everything they know to get free of a certain sin area or certain negative circumstances. They pray, fast, and cry out to God. They repent, plead the blood, and confess the Word. But the circumstances don't change. So they are about to conclude that the Word doesn't work and God is not faithful.

This is the case of many Christians trapped in the futility of their minds, darkened in their understanding, and excluded from the life of God in certain areas. They do not consider that their hearts could be hardened, because they are unaware of any willful disobedience to God. This is the "ignorance" of Ephesians 4:18. A mode of fleshly operation, deeply established in a Christian's heart and "confirmed" through many words and experiences over time, will be hardened in the person's heart and is often not instantly eradicated and replaced with the truth. Through repentance, the cleansing power of the blood of Jesus, and the washing of the water of the Word, these hardened grooves of fleshly operation can be softened, made malleable and moldable, and can be reshaped according to the truth in the spirit. Praise the Lord!

Chapter Seven:
The First Mode
of Fleshly Operation

Let's now examine the characteristics of the first mode of walking in the flesh.

This is the mode which is characterized as follows:

Experience of Fear		Experience of Self
Identity	Welfare	Plumb Line
No Value	Needs Not Met	Self-Image
1. Conscious	Unconscious	Nobody
		hope-victory-winner

When walking in this mode of flesh, a Christian believes: "I'm unimportant, not loved, and a nobody. But I can ultimately become a somebody and have victory and success in life through my service for God."

To understand a Christian walking in the flesh in this first mode, let's consider an imaginary man named Bill. He has received deep in his soul the message that God doesn't really love him. Therefore, he considers himself to have little value and importance. He sees himself according to this message and always perceives others as more important and blessed of God than he.

No matter what status or position he attains in the world, or in the Kingdom of God, Bill always feels unimportant and unappreciated. He feels that he is not really honored and esteemed by others and, ultimately, by God. After Bill met the Lord and began to grow in his relationship with God, he always felt unworthy of God's grace and blessing. Even when God poured out great blessing on Bill, because of his feelings of unworthiness, he had difficulty receiving it. When Bill was not experiencing God's blessing, usually he believed it stemmed from unworthiness and inability to please God.

However, Bill sometimes became frustrated and believed he had done enough to be worthy of God's blessing. Yet God unfairly and unjustly "withheld" blessing from Bill.

Bill does not consciously experience the fear that his needs will not be met. Nonetheless, the fear regarding his personal welfare motivates Bill through his flesh without his conscious-awareness. Because he doesn't consciously experience this fear, Bill has hope for the future. He expects to be successful and victorious in life because of his obedience to the Lord and his ability to win God's favor and blessing through that obedience.

Because Bill feels that God and others don't really value or esteem him as they should, pride motivates him to exalt himself above others and make himself important in the eyes of God and others. Rebellion usually operates through Bill in a hidden, covert way as he outwardly appears to be compliant and submissive.

Operation in this particular mode of the flesh tends to affect Bill's self-image as follows: "I'm not really a very valuable or important person, but I want to be, and I will be. If I am diligent, submissive, and obedient to the Lord, I'll do great things in the Kingdom of God and become a valuable and important person."

We can see that Bill is not receiving the fact that he is already loved and accepted unconditionally by God, because the blood of Jesus Christ cleansed his spirit and made him holy and acceptable in the spirit. Bill has received the lie that says, "I can earn God's love and esteem to create personal value through works of obedience" (Titus 3:5).

Walking in the flesh in this particular way generates the following perception of Bill's relationship with God: "He doesn't really value me. No matter how hard I try or what I do, God doesn't really acknowledge or bless me. I long to hear Him say, 'Well done, thou good and faithful servant', but He never does. As a matter of fact, it seems that God blesses others who aren't even obedient to Him. You would think that all my years of service to God would be worth something, but God never seems to acknowledge me. However, if I press on serving Him, God will have to acknowledge me. At least I will receive my reward in heaven."

Bill views God as being somewhat unfair. Bill is convinced, subconsciously, that God's love, acceptance, and blessing are predicated upon performance. God seems somewhat unfair because *no matter what Bill does*, he can never seem to please God and be acknowledged for his service by God. This is the lie. His focus is on performance, yet he believes that he is simply trusting God and being obedient to Him. The fact is, Bill is not trusting God. He is trusting in himself, and he is driven by pride in his flesh to perform in order to "win" God's love and approval.

A Christian walking in this mode of flesh usually perceives his personal value to be in his job or ministry. He actually, however, experiences a deep sense of not being valued, honored, or esteemed by God or others. Pride manifests itself quite overtly in this person as he strives for importance through his career or ministry.

This believer tends to see other authorities in his life and those close to him in the same way that he views God. He will have a great tendency to compare himself with other Christians. He keeps score with others privately and makes certain he is winning. (He would probably never admit this to anyone.) In order to feel good about himself, he must make sure that he is performing better than others around him with whom he privately competes in the areas where he can excel.

This person will tend to judge his parents for not esteeming and appreciating him. He then has an expectancy that others in his life also will not respect, esteem, or appreciate him. If he marries, he will expect his spouse not to appreciate or honor him. He may even compete with his spouse spiritually, or otherwise, and exalt himself by putting his spouse down to compensate for the worthlessness inside. While doing so, he expects everyone around him to value and esteem him for his performance and works, but they rarely do.

When they don't do so, this person is irritated but believes the must press on: "One day I will be acknowledged and appreciated." Very often, this person unwittingly manipulates others around him in order to draw attention to his own works so that he will be honored.

In general, this person will draw near to authorities in his life and try to win their esteem and acceptance through performing to please them. Because he believes that this is how personal value is obtained, it is difficult for him to receive love, acceptance, and esteem from others except on the basis of having earned it.

Because the feeling of being unimportant is consciously present, degrees and titles are usually important to this person. External appearance can also be important. Automobiles, houses, other material possessions, and wealth can be important because this person believes that such things evoke esteem and honor from others.

Commonly, a person walking in the flesh in this mode can become a workaholic and neglect his family because acceptance, esteem, and honor come through performance, and his family does not appreciate him anyway. Many pastors and spiritual leaders operate in this mode of fleshly thought and behavior. They are drawn to become pastors and spiritual leaders in the first place in an attempt to *do* something important for God and thereby win His love and favor. They don't realize they already have God's love and acceptance because of a conscious feeling of having little value in His sight.

Women operating in this mode have a greater tendency to become anorexic or bulimic than those walking in any other mode. They feel worthless. They focus on appearance as ascribing value to them. They are not in total despair, but believe that they can personally control their circumstances and physical bodies in order to become loved. Walking in these lies of the devil then leads toward anorexia and/or bulimia. This person *must* win in the areas of performance in which he has chosen to compete. If they are not measuring up to their own expectations, or are being beaten by others, they must *do* something about it in order to win. They have to try harder. In the case of anorexia, their own body is the focus.

Let's look in the Word at an example of someone living substantially in this first mode of fleshly living.

"But the father said to his slaves, 'Quickly bring out the best robe and put it on him, and put a ring on his hand and sandals on his feet; and bring the fattened calf, kill it, let us eat and be merry; for this son of mine was dead, and has been found' and they began to be merry. Now his older son was in the field, and when he came home and approached the house, he heard music and dancing. "And he summoned one of the servants and began inquiring what these things might be. And he said to him, 'Your brother has come and your father has received him back safe and sound'. But he became angry, and was not willing to go in: and his father came out and began entreating him. But he answered and said to his father, 'Look! For so many years I have been serving you, and I have never neglected a command of yours; and yet you have never given me a kid, that I might be merry with my friends; but when this son of yours came, who has devoured your wealth with harlots, you killed the fattened calf for him.' And he said to him, 'My child, you have always been with me, and all that is mine is yours. But we had to be merry and rejoice for this brother of yours was dead and has begun to live, and was lost and has been found'" (Luke 15:22-33).

You'll undoubtedly recognize this as Jesus' parable of the prodigal son. In this instance, we are not going to look at the prodigal son, but at his older brother who was walking in this first mode of fleshly behavior.

Jesus told the parable primarily to demonstrate God's unconditional love toward His children. This love is revealed through the father's love of the younger son whose performance was abominable. It was this very point that the older brother could not understand or accept. In his mind, he was never able to receive the unconditional love of his father. He was convinced that love, acceptance, esteem and honor were, and ought to be, conditional upon obedience and performance.

In this parable, Jesus didn't tell us very much about

the childhood of these two brothers. But based upon the results we see in their adulthood, I would imagine that these two brothers probably competed strongly with one another for their father's love and attention. The older, however, always had to win. He was probably good at most of the things he chose to do. The younger must have felt as though he could not compete with his brother. Undoubtedly, the big brother was ruthless in his compulsion to be better than his brother at everything and, thereby, win his father's love and esteem.

Both brothers believed the lie that love and acceptance from their father came from performance. However, as these boys grew up together, the younger saw that if winning his father's love and attention meant he had to outdo his brother, there was no way he could win. He tried, but his brother seized every opportunity to put him down and exalt himself. The younger brother simply slipped into the mode of living based on the conscious experience of current death and fear of future death in the realm of personal identity and welfare.

The older brother felt of little value, but, because he was driven to perform, he believed that one day his father would take notice of his obedience, and he would be acknowledged. He continued drawing near to his father in attempts to win love and attention.

If his father said, "Work eight hours in the field," the brother worked ten so that his diligence would be acknowledged. No matter how hard he worked, however, or what he did to demonstrate his loyalty, he was never acknowledged.

Then the younger brother returned home after squandering the family fortune in sin.

The father received him back with joy, acknowledging him, showering him with love, honoring him like a foreign dignitary by having a huge feast and killing the fattened calf. To the older son, who thoroughly believed that esteem and honor should come based on performance, this was the ultimate insult and slap in the face from his father.

The subtle rebellion of rejecting his father's love and trusting in his own abilities to meet his own needs obviously had not worked.

Compelled now by intensified fear, this older brother's hope of success and becoming a somebody was slipping away. He saw he was doomed to failure with his father and that he could never win his father's esteem and honor, no matter what he did. Therefore, he concluded that it was futile to try anymore. Thus, he slipped from mode one to mode three.

Subtle rebellion hadn't worked, so as fear intensified, he lost hope, moved into mode three and tried more intensified open rebellion. He refused to go to the feast and then blatantly opposed his father to his face.

When fear intensifies, as it did at this point with this young man, the only way that our flesh can deal with it is to attempt self-exaltation in pride or opposition in rebellion or both! This young man did both! He was consumed with anger and hatred when his father freely poured out, on the "worthless" brother, honor, love and esteem, for which the older son strived all of his life. In rebellion, he withdrew from the relationship and decided that he just wouldn't relate to his father anymore.

He refused to go inside to the feast. But the father, who loved the son, sought him outside.

In pride, this son verbally exalted himself before his father and recounted all his diligent service, righteous deeds and obedience. The first word said to the father is "Look", as if to say "Don't you see? Are you blind? You ascribe honor and esteem to harlotry and drunkenness, but not to obedience, loyalty, and diligent work."

Do you see how the serpent in this son's heart had established false plumb line images that robbed him of receiving his father's love? Because of the fear that he was of no value and that his need would not be met, especially his need to feel significant, he had missed out all his life on the very thing for which he had longed: "He who seeks to save his life, shall lose it."

When the truth was revealed that the father's love

was unconditional, not dependent upon performance, instead of receiving the truth, repenting and being set free, the son changed to a different mode of pride and rebellion and justified himself in it.

He decided that the first mode of walking in the flesh wasn't working, so he intensified pride and rebellion to deal with the hurt, and frustration by moving to the third mode of flesh. When one mode of pride and rebellion doesn't work, often our flesh motivates us to try another mode.

It could be that this son then told others how unfairly his father had treated him. Because of the serpent in his flesh, and the lie that love and honor come on the basis of performance, he would have continued to relate to God, an employer, a spouse, close friends and others on the same basis upon which he related to his father. It would always have seemed to him that he was never appreciated and that others did not value him as they should. These people would become, for him, "lions" and "bears." As long as he continues not to receive revelation from God of the snake and the false plumb lines, he would continue allowing his flesh to rule. His needs would remain unmet and he would always believe that his problems came because other people were wrong and treated him unfairly when, in actuality, the problems were because of the poison of the serpent in his soul.

I was recounting in earlier chapters about Steve, a minister friend who had judged his father and others for treating him unfairly. Steve judged "the system" and certain other ministries for being insensitive to people's needs. He then reaped the fruit of those judgments in his own life, his family and his ministry.

However, we can see that these judgments proceeded from the established mode in which his flesh had operated for years. Steve was unaware of his flesh governing his soul in this way, but he was, in fact, operating in the same fleshly mode as the older brother in Luke 15.

Because of the conscious feeling of having little value, pride was operating through Steve's flesh to exalt himself in God's eyes and the eyes of others. He also, unknowingly, believed that love, esteem, and honor were given on the basis of performance.

Thus, Steve was compelled and driven by fear to work long hours in ministry. Steve really became a "ministryaholic" for Jesus, and believed that he was being diligent and obedient to the Lord in doing so. He didn't realize that he wasn't being motivated to such service by the Spirit of God in his spirit, but by his flesh striving to win the love and esteem of God and others around him.

Steve frequently over-committed himself to others, because he wanted to please them and be sensitive to their needs. Sometimes he would tell someone, "I'll call you," when he knew, even as he said it, that his schedule would not permit him to do so. His flesh deceived him into believing that he could just tell the person later that he could not fulfill the commitment.

He was, in fact, lying to people because he did not want to disappoint them or appear that he didn't care about them. This all came from the underlying false image that he was not esteemed and honored by God or others and was unimportant and had little value.

The primary difference between Steve and the prodigal son's brother is that when Steve heard the truth about his flesh governing him in this way, he didn't reject it and react in greater pride and rebellion, or change modes. Instead, he went to his Heavenly Father and asked Him to reveal to him the truth of the matter. As Steve prayed, the Holy Spirit revealed to him the operation of the serpent within him. He repented, asked the Lord's forgiveness, and began to allow his mind to be renewed to the truth.

However, a person may instead decide to harden his heart, continue operating in the same mode, and try all the harder to win love and esteem through good works. This person may choose to "repent" into another mode of fleshly domination.

He could slide into the self-pity and withdrawal or

open rebellion of mode three. In this case, he would say, "I know how diligent and obedient and righteous I have been, and I don't care if God or anyone else acknowledges me. I know that I deserve honor and esteem." He would then rebel against those who had hurt him by either terminating relationships and refusing to relate, blatantly opposing them, or doing both.

When negative pressure or circumstances arise against the person whose flesh is operating through them in the first mode, they can react in several different ways. The correct way, of course, is to go to the Lord and ask God for revelation of how the serpent in our flesh may have deceived us and caused us to sow something in the flesh, the results of which we may now be reaping. As we receive revelation, we can repent of an entire mode of operation and begin to be purged, cleansed and healed.

Chapter Eight:
The Second Mode
of Fleshly Operation

This second mode is characterized as follows:

Experience of Fear		Experience of Self
Identity	Welfare	Plumb Line
No Value	Needs Not Met	Self-Image
2. Unconscious	Unconscious	Somebody
		hope-victory-winner

When walking in this mode of flesh, a Christian believes: "I am important and valuable. I am a somebody — because of who I am and what I do. I can remain a somebody by continuing what I'm doing now and by doing even greater things in the future. I will have victory in my life and be a success." Let's call the Christian walking in this second mode "Sue."

Sue has received, deep inside her soul, the message that God doesn't really love her, and, therefore, her life isn't valuable and her needs won't be met. However, she is not consciously aware of these two fears operating through her. She believes that she is a valuable, worthwhile, and important person. Sue says that this is because of Jesus in her and verbally gives God the credit for success in her life. The truth is that she feels valuable because of who she is, and what she has done, and what she is doing.

Unknowingly, Sue has placed trust and confidence in herself. However, she thinks that she is placing it in Jesus Christ and she is trusting in God's Word. She is actually trusting in her own ability to understand God's Word. She thinks that she is trusting in God's revelation to her, but she is actually trusting in her own ability to receive revelation from God. She thinks that she is trusting in Jesus' righteousness within her. She trusts in her own ability to walk righteously. These seem to be subtle differences, but they are really the difference between trusting in God and trusting in self.

Because Sue is walking in this second mode of fleshly dominion, she perceives her relationship with God as follows: "God is pleased with me. God does honor, esteem and value me. He is blessing me." She believes that God is treating her fairly and says with her mouth that His blessing on her life is due to His love and mercy. But she really believes in her heart that it is due to her own righteousness and obedience to God.

Sue appears to others to be very secure and self confident. She also experiences herself to be this way. She thinks of herself as being confident and competent. She has no conscious awareness of the fear that her needs won't be met, because she usually experiences most of her needs being met in a substantial measure. Because of her confidence and competence, Sue is getting her needs met. She is a self starter and initiator who doesn't wait for things to happen. She makes them happen. In reality, Sue often mistakes the creativity of her own natural mind for the leading of the Holy Spirit.

Like the Christian operating in the first mode, Sue frequently compares herself with others. Sue also must make certain that she is superior to the others with whom she has chosen to compete. Because her value as a person is determined in her mind by achievement, Sue is driven by her flesh to excel in every area where she has chosen to endeavor. In general, she simply won't endeavor to compete or achieve in areas where she isn't quite certain (in advance) that she can win.

The person operating in this second mode usually appears quite successful to others. He often remains aloof from others and doesn't really open up to share his true feelings. He will discuss visions and projects with others, but he is usually unwilling to make himself vulnerable for others to see who he really is. He is afraid to let others see any areas where he is not competent or confident, because he needs to feel superior to others around him in order not to experience fear of death of his personal identity. Others are often intimidated by this air of "confidence and competitiveness" that surrounds the person operating in this mode.

This Christian is always very busy accomplishing "the Lord's work." It is very easy for him to "bulldoze" right through others whom he perceives to be in the way of accomplishing "God's purposes." He's usually quite insensitive to the needs of others, because he is driven to achievement and is focused on the accomplishment of goals. Because this person is compelled to achieve, and must excel beyond others around him, he often hurts the feeling of others close to him and causes them to feel that he doesn't care about them.

This Christian can be quite critical of others and is frequently sarcastic. His humor is usually at someone else's expense. He constantly manipulates people and circumstances, chiefly by subtly putting others down through humor, criticism, and sarcasm for the purpose of exalting himself above others. This person is usually optimistic, and rarely depressed.

The person operating in this second mode of fleshly control does not experience the fear of having no value. Consequently, pride motivates him to trust in himself and his achievements to bring him value and esteem.

Rebellion usually operates through this person in an overt, non-hidden way. Because he believes he is a some-body, if he is opposed or treated "unfairly," he will blatantly oppose or flee from the relationship in rebellion.

In general, this person will draw near to authorities in his life because he is usually able to please them and win their favor and esteem through his accomplishments. He expects other people to esteem him, because he consciously believes that he is of value and worthy of esteem, and usually they do.

Around the time that Jesus walked on earth, there lived a Jewish man in Palestine who was dominated by this second mode of fleshly operation. As this man grew up, he was driven by pride to excel in every area of his endeavors. The deepest desire of his heart was to serve God and be the best for his God. This man considered himself especially blessed, because he was not only a Jew, one of God's chosen, but he also came from a very prominent Jewish family, from one of the leading tribes and had been born into a family that was holy and kept the law. All the proper ordinances of circumcision, bar mitzvah and other Jewish rights and commandments of the law had been performed in this man's family at just the proper time and in the proper ways. His family had seen to it that he was lacking in no area of importance. This man, no doubt, felt very fortunate to have been from the nation of God's chosen people from a leading tribe, from a very prestigious family, having been trained to keep the law of God since birth, and not only this, he had also been granted Roman citizenship.

This man had everything going for him. It was no wonder that, when he grew up, he quickly excelled beyond all his contemporaries. He felt that he was not just a person who was very lucky and got all the breaks. He created the breaks. This man didn't just sit around and wait for doors to open for him, but he took all the necessary steps and created the open doors. He quickly became a leading Pharisee in all of Judea, extremely zealous for God and for the upholding of God's law.

Considering himself superior in all respects, this man found himself more righteous, more zealous, more learned, more creative, more determined, and he accomplished more in his life than most of his contemporaries. If this were not so, he would have done whatever were necessary to see that it were.

After the resurrection of Jesus, when this man became acquainted with followers of Jesus who promoted the idea that righteousness came through Jesus' atonement and not through the Jewish law, he became determined in his heart to totally annihilate such teaching and the people who followed it. He truly believed that this group of Christians was attempting to destroy, and draw people away from everything that was good, right, holy, and precious.

This man's personal identity and value was being challenged by the teaching of Christians, because, deep inside, he doubted God's love for him, and had trusted in his position and achievements to bring him value, esteem, and honor. As this was challenged by the followers of Jesus, the fear of not being of value and of having his needs unmet became more intense. Consequently, pride and rebellion rose up in him in greater intensity as he sought to exalt himself, his beliefs, and his "party" against the Christians. In rebellion, he blatantly opposed the Christians and vowed to exterminate them. Undoubtedly the Holy Spirit was speaking to this man even during this time, but he was unable to hear God due to the pride and rebellion working within.

Eventually this man was born again as he met Jesus in a vision on the road to Damascus. He, of course, was the Apostle Paul. In the third chapter of his letter to the Philippians, he describes his former trust and confidence in his own abilities, status, and achievements.

"Although I myself might have confidence even in the flesh. If anyone else has a mind to put confidence in the flesh, I far more; circumcised the eighth day, of the nation of Israel, of the tribe of Benjamin, a Hebrew of Hebrews; as to the Law, a Pharisee; as to zeal, a persecutor of the church; as to the righteousness which is in the Law, found blameless" (Philippians 3:4-6).

In verses 7-9, Paul tells us how he repented of this entire mode of fleshly operation. He counted these things in which he had formerly trusted as rubbish. He quit identifying himself at all with his former life and sought to identify himself only according to the truth of who God had recreated him to be in the spirit. He had come to know, experience, and trust in God's love for him.

In spite of Paul's new birth and substantial soulical renewal, however, there still remained a mode of fleshly operation based on the former false plumb line image in which he continued to operate from time to time. The primary characteristic of this mode of walking in the flesh was exaltation of self in pride, through trusting in himself and his own abilities and status. We see this serpent still operating through Paul bringing death in certain areas of his life in 2 Corinthians 12:7-9.

> *"And because of the surpassing greatness of the revelations, for this reason, to keep me from exalting myself, there was given me a thorn in the flesh, a messenger of Satan to buffet me — to keep me from exalting myself! Concerning this I entreated the Lord three times that it might depart from me. And He has said to me, 'My grace is sufficient for you, for* **power is perfected in weakness.'** *Most gladly, therefore, I will rather boast about my weaknesses, that the power of Christ may dwell in me."*

Paul received tremendous revelation from God. However, he then slipped into an old groove, still present in his heart, motivating him to believe that he really was more special than other people to receive such revelation. He began to believe that this revelation came due to his status as Paul the Apostle, and his tremendous obedience, righteousness and zeal for God. This pride that Paul allowed to operate became the door through which a messenger of Satan came and harassed him.

So we see that, even as long and intensely as Paul had walked with the Lord, he was still subject to being deceived by the serpent in his flesh and drawn out of the spirit, allowing his soul to be captured and dominated by his flesh. It was the same false plumb line — fear — and prideful reaction to fear, that had operated through him before he was born again.

This second mode of walking in the flesh can sometimes be quite subtle and others around someone operating in this mode may not discern that he is walking unknowingly in the flesh. They may be deceived themselves and think that such a person is in the spirit. Truly great spiritual leaders walk in this mode and conduct parts of their ministry in this mode of fleshly domain more than any other mode.

When negative pressure is applied to a Christian walking in this second mode of flesh, thereby intensifying fear, such a person will intensify pride and rebellion to deal with the fear and hurt. However, he may also attempt to abandon this second mode and try any of the other three modes. If such person continues to believe he is right and righteous, but the circumstances, God, others or the devil are too powerful for him to win, he may give up and move into the fourth mode.

Let's look at another Old Testament example of a person operating in this second mode.

"Though I am righteous, my mouth will condemn me: Though I am guiltless, He will declare me guilty" (Job 9:20).

Job declares here that he is righteous and it is God who is unrighteous because He condemns the guiltless. Due to the affliction that befell Job, fear greatly intensified and pride and rebellion correspondingly intensified. Not only this, but Job decided that the second mode wasn't adequately coping with the situation and decided to try the fourth mode. Throughout most of the book of Job, we find him speaking out of great pride and rebellion believing that he is righteous and good and is a somebody because of it, but that he can't win and be successful. He thought that God was unfair, unjust, and far more powerful than he. Job believed that God was the one afflicting him. We know, of course, that it was not God, but Satan who was bringing death and destruction to Job's life. Van Gayle has written an excellent book. *Job — A Story of Redemption*[1] which I highly recommend to anyone with questions on this subject.

Before the affliction, I believe that the 29th chapter of Job reveals how Job was walking in the flesh according to the second mode. He believed that he was a somebody and that his trust in himself was bearing fruit. Job was currently successful and had a hope and expectation for continued future success and victory. The following verses of chapter 29 reveal how Job used to perceive himself and his life before the affliction.

"When His lamp shone over my head, and by His light I walked through darkness; As I was in the prime of my days, When the friendship of God was over my tent; For when the ear heard, it called me blessed; and when the eye saw, it gave witness of me, Because I delivered the poor who cried for help, and the orphan who had no helper. The blessing of the one ready to perish came upon me, and I made the widow's heart sing for joy. I put on righteousness, and it clothed me; My justice was like a robe and a turban. I was eyes to the blind, and feet to the lame. I was a father to the needy, and I investigated the case which I did not know. And I broke the jaws of the wicked, and snatched the prey from his teeth. Then I thought, 'I shall die in my nest, and I shall multiply my days as the sand. My root is spread out to the waters, and dew lies all night on my branch. My glory is ever new with me, and my bow is renewed in my hand.' To me they listened and waited, and kept silent for my counsel. After my words they did not speak again, and my speech dropped on them. And they waited for me as for the rain, and opened their mouth as for the spring rain. I smiled on them when they did not believe, and the light of my face they did not cast down. I chose a way for them and sat as chief, and dwelt as a king among the troops, as one who comforted the mourners" (Job 29:3-4, 11-25).

Job had experienced tremendous success before the affliction. He was a wealthy ruler who ministered to the needs of many others. All of this was rooted in pride, but Job thought that it was righteousness before God.

Chapter 30 reveals the bitter root judgment in which Job walked toward others before the affliction and then its fruit during his affliction.

*"But now those younger than I mock me, **Whose fathers I disdained to put with the dogs of my flock.** Indeed, what good was the strength of their hands to me? Vigor had perished from them. From want and famine they are gaunt Who gnaw the dry ground by night in waste and desolation, Who plucks mallow by the bushes, and whose food is the root of the broom shrub. They are driven from the community; They shout against them as against a thief, So that they dwell in dreadful valleys, In holes of*

*the earth and of the rocks. Among the bushes they cry out; Under the nettles they are gathered together. Fools, even those without a name, they were scourged from the land. **And now I have become their taunt,** I have even become a byword to them. They abhor me and stand aloof from me, and they do not refrain from spitting at my face. Because He has loosed His bowstring and afflicted me, They have cast off the bridle before me" (Job 30:1-11).*

Job's accusers were not taunting him because God had loosed His bowstring and afflicted him. Job was simply reaping the consequences of the judgment that he had sown. He had treated other men as being the scum of the earth, not even worthy of living with his sheepdogs. Job was now reaping the fruit of that judgment. He was experiencing the death that is always brought on by walking in the flesh.

In chapter 42, Job finally received revelation knowledge from God and repented. All during the affliction he had attempted to "figure out" the solution using natural, logical reasoning. He had interpreted the circumstances wrongly and, of course, drawn wrong conclusions. Finally, in verses 5 and 6 of chapter 42, he received revelation from God. For the first time, Job saw the true image of God and himself through revelation in the spirit. Before, he had only seen and heard of God through a false image in his natural mind.

"I have heard of Thee by the hearing ear; But now my eye sees Thee; Therefore I retract, and I repent in dust and ashes" (Job 42:5-6).

I am very familiar, personally, with this second mode of walking in the flesh because the Lord has shown me that it is the mode through which sin in my flesh has tended to operate. In the first chapter, I shared an experience I had in which the Lord began to deal with me about my criticism of others. I learned later that this was not an isolated manifestation of my flesh, but only a superficial manifestation of an entire mode of walking in the flesh. The critical words were rooted in pride operating through me without my conscious awareness.

The pride was a fleshly reaction to my fear of having no value and ultimately, not being loved by God.

The lie I told to Christy about my meeting with Marilyn and the lie I wanted to make up to tell Jan about why I was late were both superficial manifestations of my walking in the flesh and were a result of the repeated poisoning of my soul by the serpent. This had resulted in false plumb line images which were now hardened in my heart. This was the revelation that the Lord unfolded to me through my friend, Jean, when we were traveling in Poland. As she described the way I had been bulldozing over my wife, teaching the Word in my own strength and wisdom, speaking critically of others and generally operating in a lot of pride, the Lord began to unfold this entire mode of operation of my flesh.

When I saw the truth of my operation in these things, I began to ask the Lord to reveal to me how my flesh had captured my soul, motivating me to walk in the flesh trusting in myself, thinking I was trusting in God.

The Lord showed me that when I was a very small child, I learned not to trust other people to meet my needs. I decided that if something were to get done and my goals were to be met, I was the best person to rely upon. I had decided that I had no need to rely upon, or trust other people, but that I, myself, was more reliable and trustworthy than anyone else to accomplish my goals and purposes, which, since being born again, I now believed were God's goals and purposes.

The Lord showed me that, in pride, I had looked down on and despised others who were not competent and confident in the same areas I was confident. In order not to consciously experience lack of value and worth-lessness, pride had driven me all my life to be the best at whatever I chose to do. If I could be the best, then I could remain exalted (in pride) above all others in my own eyes and (so I thought) in the eyes of others. Consequently, I found out that it was easier to compete and be the best if I chose to do exotic things.

In junior high school, I spent many hours becoming

a competent sailplane pilot and soaring over the Rocky Mountains. No one else in my school even knew how to fly a glider, so I was the best. In high school, I spent my free time skydiving, hot air ballooning, and flying. Few others my age could compete with me in these areas.

The Lord revealed to me that, all my life, I had simply avoided areas where I couldn't excel through my own natural ability. I chose more exotic pursuits where there was less competition. This was motivated by pride and trust in myself as a reaction to the fear of being not honored and esteemed, and being of no value. I had been able to create value and esteem for myself in the eyes of others through my own "clever" ideas and abilities.

The Lord showed me that, after I was born again, this same mode of fleshly living continued in my life and now extended into my walk with the Lord. Because I had never really learned to trust or rely on others, and had thought that I was more competent and reliable than anyone else to meet my needs and goals, I didn't trust in or rely on the Lord either. I had always thought that I was trusting in Him, but the Lord showed me that I was trusting in my own insights and abilities. I was still choosing exotic areas of ministry (behind the Iron Curtain, etc.) so that others could be impressed.

I am not saying that God showed me that ministry in Eastern Europe, learning Russian, flying, or any of these other activities were wrong. He just spoke to me that the motivations in my heart for pursuing them were emanating from sin in my flesh rather than righteousness in my spirit. These were all motivated by my pride and desire to exalt myself, be acceptable to God and others through works, and were in reality being carried out in my soulish creativity and ability. I always had a measure of success by doing these things, and, thus, had thought that I was very spiritual and that "everything was fine."

However, as I began to look closely at the results and effectiveness of my life and ministry, I saw that the actual fruit was very limited. There was confusion and inconsistency. I had some success here and there, but no consistent results. The Holy Spirit showed me that this was because I was not relying on Him as I had thought, but was being compelled by pride to achieve and was relying on my own natural wisdom. Even when I received revelation and direction from God, I then relied upon my own wisdom and abilities to carry out the plan.

At this point the Lord spoke to me the following scriptures about my life.

> *"Who among you is wise and understanding? Let him show by his good behavior his deeds in the gentleness of wisdom. But if you have bitter jealousy and **selfish ambition** in your heart, do not be arrogant and so lie against the truth. This wisdom is not that which comes down from above, but is earthly, natural, demonic. For where jealousy and selfish ambition exist, there is disorder and every evil thing. But the wisdom from above is first pure, then peace-able, gentle, reasonable, full of mercy and good fruits, unwavering, without hypocrisy" (James 3:13-17).*

The Holy Spirit quickened to me the phrases *"selfish ambition"*, and "wisdom which is not from above" regarding how I had been living my Christian life.

As the Holy Spirit convicted me of these things, I repented of each aspect, acknowledged each as sin, asked forgiveness, and received cleansing by the blood of Jesus Christ. However, because these false images were "grooves" cut deeply into my soul, this mode of walking in the flesh did not instantly and totally disappear. Those grooves are still in the process of being filled in. My mind and emotions are still being renewed to the Truth. But praise the Lord! This entire mode of walking in the flesh has been exposed to me, and I can now walk in the light (I John 1:7), repent, and be cleansed each time that the Holy Spirit catches me walking in pride or unbelief. Before, the deception was so powerful that I didn't know I was even in the flesh. Now I am open to receive that revelation from God and He can show me when I am walking in it. Each time I see it operating and repent, I become freer and freer. Praise God for the redemptive power of the Blood of Jesus Christ.

Chapter Nine:
The Third Mode
of Fleshly Operation

The third and fourth modes of fleshly operation usually develop out of the first and second modes, respectively.

A person moves from mode-one to mode-three, or from mode-two to mode-four when fear has been sufficiently intensified to convince the person that he can't win and he won't be successful or have victory. This is how Job moved from mode-two to mode-four as fear and experience of not having his needs met intensified, due to the affliction. Often, negative circumstances create a greater intensity of fear, with accompanying intensified pride and rebellion.

While modes one and two experience needs being fairly well met and thus, rely more on pride to bring value, modes three and four experience needs not being met, have given up hope of winning and rely more on rebellion to deal with the fear.

While this is generally true, pride and rebellion are always operative, in varying degrees, in all four modes.

When a person operating in mode-one loses hope of victory and of becoming valuable, he slips into mode-three. This third mode is characterized as follows:

Experience of Fear		Experience of Self
Identity	Welfare	Plumb Line
No Value	Needs Not Met	Self-Image
1. Conscious	Conscious	Nobody, no hope-defeat-loser

When walking in the third mode of flesh, a Christian believes: "I'm unimportant, a nobody. I can't win in life. I'm always defeated by (God, "the system," myself, others, the devil, circumstances). I am doomed to this terrible life, and I'll always be a nobody. I won't win, so there is no point in trying."

The Christian walking this way feels doomed to a particular lifestyle because "that's just the way life is." This person's mind has the amazing ability to create situations with two negative alternatives. Doomed in either case — "If I do, I lose. If I don't, I lose." (i.e., "If I don't work this hard, we can't make it financially. If I continue to work his hard, my wife will divorce me.")

Let's call a Christian living in this third mode of flesh, "Karen." Karen walks under many heavy burdens. Life is not very enjoyable for her, but she believes that life is just like that. These burdens are her "cross" to bear for the Lord. She doesn't realize that these burdens are simply due to the death in her soul brought on by walking in the flesh.

The false image in which Karen walks causes her to view God as not being very pleased with her. She is not only consciously aware of being worthless, but is convinced that because of this, she deserves no better life. She, like those walking in any fleshly mode, doubts God's love and is convinced that His love and esteem come through performance. Because she hasn't performed well, and is convinced that she can't perform well enough to please God or win His love and favor, Karen is resigned to the fact that she will never be very spiritual or be blessed of God. Karen feels so rotten and terrible about herself that she is convinced that God must feel that same way about her too. She thinks, "I'm rotten and no good. I'm not righteous or spiritual. I don't deserve to be loved. God couldn't possibly love me. I've constantly blown it. I'm sure the negative circumstances in my life are due to God punishing me for not being more spiritual and obedient."

Ultimately, Karen may quit trying to relate to the Lord because she thinks, "He never helps me, so what's the use of trying?" Satan, operating through this mode of fleshly thinking, has greater opportunity to lead a person into alcoholism, drug addiction, and suicide than through any other mode.

Very often, people who live in this mode had a very domineering father or mother who was often arbitrary and rarely pleased with them. Frequently, they may also have grown up with a brother or sister operating in modes one or two, who was compelled to achieve and win, often at their siblings' expense. Usually the Christian walking in this mode of flesh feels that God always blesses and helps other people, but never him. He concludes that God just doesn't love, or even like him, and it's no wonder; he doesn't like himself.

Karen perceives herself as worthless, weak, and a doormat for others to wipe their feet on. She operates in a lot of guilt, condemnation and, consequently, self-pity. Deep inside is a fierce anger toward God and others who keep "rejecting and hurting" her. Her trust is not in God, because God "never blesses her or helps her." Her trust is in herself, which puts her in great fear, because she has experienced many times that she is worthless, incompetent, and incapable of meeting her own needs.

Karen is, deep inside, very angry and full of blame toward God and others for her poor circumstances. This anger is rooted in rebellion and is the fleshly mechanism for dealing with the guilt and fear. Most of the time she perceives herself and represents herself to others as a victim of circumstances and of other people or God. Her emotions are usually quite volatile, and she is subject to flying off into a rage or, perhaps, into deep depression and self-pity. Karen is frequently found complaining and is rarely pleased by others close to her.

Identifying with her flesh, Karen sees most other people as of much greater value and importance than herself. She feels that other Christians are more spiritual and closer to God. She feels inferior in many ways to most other people, and she absolutely refuses to compete with others in any area, because she doesn't want to risk another defeat. If someone attempts to draw her into competition or encourage her to try something new, she will withdraw and quit, or terminate the relationship entirely.

Karen is perceived by most other people as being quiet and reserved. She doesn't open up much to others. This is generally true of those who walk in this mode of flesh, but not always. They may sometimes appear outgoing and loud, and often they stave others off through humor and jokes. In any case, they don't allow anyone to get very close to them, lest the other find out how rotten and despicable they really are and reject them. They are greatly afraid that if anyone finds out who they really are, they will be disliked, just as they dislike themselves. This expectation of being rejected is the very mechanism used to draw negative treatment out of others.

Because Karen is starving for love and esteem, she frequently demands love and attention from others with whom she is engaged in relationship, but is unwilling to commit herself to them or really open up, for fear of being hurt. She says to others through her attitudes and actions, "Prove that you really love me unconditionally, and I'll open up to you and love you too." This demand for unconditional love from others causes others to feel uncomfortable and scares them away. Often, as Karen has done this, others experienced fear, reacted in rebellion, and fled from the relationship, once again confirming to Karen her expectation of not being liked and being a victim of the cruelty of others.

Jesus truly is the only one who can provide a person with unconditional love 100 percent of the time. Looking to others for the love that only God can provide is motivated by pride, a search to gain respect, esteem and love from others in a vain attempt to fill the terrible vacuum of worthlessness and fear inside the soul.

Rebellion operates powerfully through Karen, causing her to withdraw from God and others and flee from all potentially hurtful relationships. She appears meek and withdrawn to others, and most of the time rebellion operates in her in a hidden, covert way. Because Karen feels like a nobody, she feels unworthy to blatantly oppose anyone. She's also not interested in being shot down or defeated anymore. Instead, Karen usually just withdraws and retreats from relationships. Even when the Lord gently trys to draw her back into relationship with Him, the fear is so intense that she usually rebels against the Lord and backs further away.

Karen even receives condemnation from reading the Bible. One time when she hadn't read the Word for three or four months, Karen decided to try to get up early and have a quiet time with the Lord. She felt somewhat guilty about having been out of the Word for so long, but she decided to try. She got up and thought, "Let's see. Where should I read? I need something cheerful and encouraging. I know. Psalms. That's usually encouraging. I'll start with Psalm 1. 'How blessed is the man who does not walk in the counsel of the wicked, nor stands in the path of sinners, nor sits in the seat of scoffers! But his delight is in the law of the Lord, and in His law he meditates day and night.'"

She then thinks, "I guess that's why I'm not blessed. I am wicked. I am a sinner, and I'm probably a scoffer too. My delight isn't in the Word because I haven't read it for three months, and I don't meditate in it day and night. No wonder my life is a mess. I'm rotten. God couldn't love someone who doesn't even read His Word and who sure doesn't delight in it."

Karen ends up feeling depressed and discouraged, and she gives up on reading for another three months. No one likes to receive guilt and condemnation. In truth, this reaction is rebellion operating through her flesh, reacting to the fear of death and, in result, creating the soulish death that she feared. This proves that pride and rebellion always bring death to the soul.

Earlier, in several chapters, I referred to a woman, Terry, who came for counseling regarding a business decision, but discovered she was angry at God for not providing her with a husband. Terry had been walking in the flesh according to this third mode, but didn't realize it. This mode of operation caused her to expect men who could be potential husbands to reject her and terminate the relationship.

Because she didn't really believe that she was valuable and worth loving Terry expected that others would also view her that way. In her attempt to draw love and attention out of a man to whom she was relating, she would end up scaring him away.

While traveling overseas, I counseled with Larry, who had been walking in this mode. Larry, who had been born again for about a year, had, for some time, been involved in karate. Through his study of karate, Larry had opened his soul to affliction by a demonic spirit that would occasionally seize control of Larry and throw him into an uncontrollable rage. He was afraid that one day he would unknowingly kill someone in this rage. Many times Larry had received prayer for deliverance from this spirit, but it never left him.

As we talked, Larry explained more about his life. He was about 19 years old and he been living with his girlfriend without being married for three or four years. They had both been born again almost a year previously. At that time, the Holy Spirit convicted them both that they were to be married. But first they were to terminate their illicit sexual relationship until after the marriage. They had been under the conviction for eight months, but had done nothing about it until only a month prior to our meeting. Larry had felt very guilty and ashamed before God that he had been so slow to obey.

Concurrently, Larry had applied to enter the university and had failed the entrance exam by only three points. Since he did not gain entrance to the university, Larry was now obligated to serve in the Army and would be inducted shortly. On top of all this, it now appeared that his girlfriend was pregnant.

Poor Larry felt like a man being constantly chased by lions and bears. He was certain that all of his negative circumstances were God's punishment for his disobedience. He also believed that this was why God wouldn't deliver him from the demonic spirit that was afflicting him. Certain he had lost his salvation, Larry asked me what he needed to do to have his name rewritten in the Book of Life. Feeling so worthless and ashamed before God, Larry couldn't come to the Lord because he was sure that God felt about him the same way that he felt about himself. This was further confirmed by God's "lack of help" and all the increasing negative circumstances.

As I ministered God's love to Larry, the truth of who he was in the spirit, and the power of the blood of Jesus, he began to receive some hope. Then he repented from fear of his Heavenly Father and asked to be cleansed by the blood of Jesus. While we were praying, he saw a vision of the literal blood of Jesus being poured into the top of his head and flowing down through his body until it had purged and cleansed every cell.

After receiving this vision, Larry said, "I feel completely clean!" He now knew that he was holy, righteous and pure *in his spirit*, because of the blood of Jesus. I told Larry, "You have authority in the name of Jesus to command that demonic spirit to depart from you permanently." Larry did so and felt a tremendous release.

"Larry," I said, "you can trust the Lord for your welfare, and be sure that God did not create those negative circumstances. If you trust in the Lord, the circumstances can all be changed completely and you can have victory in each of them."

Three months later, I had an opportunity to see this same young man again. He was studying in the university and had not gone into the Army. He and his girlfriend were now married and excitedly awaiting the birth of their first child. Larry was completely free of the demonic spirit, and it hadn't bothered him at all since the time of his deliverance three months earlier.

It is somewhat common for Christians operating in this third mode of the flesh to "flip-flop" between different manifestations of pride and rebellion. They swing back and forth on a pendulum from guilt, self-pity, and condemnation to justification, self-righteousness and blame. When they are up emotionally, they operate in outward pride (arrogance) and open rebellion, and when they are down, in inward pride (self-pity) and hidden rebellion. The death, destruction, and problems continue in either case. But when a person is "up," the problems are "God's fault." When a person is "down," their problems are blamed on self.

Once I counseled a man who came into the office in deep depression and despair. Harvey was walking in tremendous death in most areas of his soul and had a deep fear of more death. He felt that God was totally against him, and that nothing he could ever do would obtain the love and favor of God. Harvey was losing many battles with overt sin in his life and felt totally guilty, condemned, and worthless.

I ministered God's love and forgiveness to Harvey, including the truth of who he was in Christ in his spirit. Harvey then repented of trusting in himself, of doubting God's love, and of fear, pride and rebellion.

However, instead of allowing his spirit to tell him the truth and govern his soul, Harvey simply changed the external manifestations of pride and rebellion and continued to blame God for all the negative circumstances in his life. But instead of feeling worthless, Harvey decided, "I deserve much better treatment than God has given me." He was praying, reading the Bible, and trying to serve God. He was doing his part. But, as far as Harvey was concerned, God was being unfaithful. Any problems were "all God's fault," because Harvey was "faithful and righteous."

As I ministered to Harvey, I pointed out the pride and rebellion that were still being manifested in Harvey's soul, just in different form. I showed him, "You are still walking in the flesh and allowing pride and rebellion to destroy your life." He then switched back, right away, to the former fleshly techniques. "You're right," he acknowledged. "No matter what I do, I can never please God or anyone else. I always fail. No wonder God can't bless me. It's all my own fault."

Fear was so intense in him that it was very difficult

for him to release control of his soul to his spirit. Each time he thought he was doing so in repentance, he was actually only repenting from certain fleshly techniques of dealing with fear to others. The fear continued to motivate him and, consequently, pride and rebellion still governed his soul through different other manifestations.

When fear is intensified in a Christian's life, if he doesn't repent and come into the spirit in faith toward God, often he may try many variations of pride and rebellion to deal with the fear, thinking he is repenting. In actuality, he is only changing the external manifestations of his flesh.

Consider again an example from Scripture of a person operating in this third mode of walking in the flesh. The prodigal son's brother was in the first mode, while the prodigal was in the third mode. Both brothers consciously felt no value, but the older brother believed that he could become valuable by winning love and esteem from his father, while the younger felt that there was no hope of winning in competition against his brother, and he thus gave up trying.

The younger brother's only way to deal with the fear of death in his soul was to escape and flee in rebellion from "death-producing" people and circumstances. He asked for his share of the inheritance and left town. In rebellion against his father and brother, he traveled as far as possible away from his family and lived a lifestyle that was totally inconsistent with his family's lifestyle.

This rebellion resulted in producing the very thing he had feared — more death in his soul, as well as poverty and slavery.

When the prodigal son finally returned to his father, he was still filled with guilt, shame, and fear. However, in this parable, Jesus gives us a very good picture of how God really views each of us, but especially the Christian who has been blatantly walking in the flesh. The father ran out to meet his son when he saw him. He didn't want the son to be embarrassed before others, so he clothed him with a fine robe, shoes, and the family signet ring of authority before anyone saw him in his original, deplorable state.

This father restored full authority to the son in the family and over money, and then honored him at a large feast in a manner suited to a foreign dignitary. This is how our Heavenly Father sees each one of us. He longs and desires to honor, esteem, and pour out His love upon us. He longs to give us life. Only the death produced by walking in the flesh prevents us, as believers, from receiving that life, and honor, and love from the Lord.

Look at one more example from the Old Testament of a man walking in this third mode of fleshly living:

"Then an angel of the Lord came and sat under the oak that was in Ophrah, which belonged to Joash the Abiezrite as his son Gideon was beating out wheat in the wine press in order to save it from the Midianites. And the angel of the Lord appeared to him and said to him, 'The Lord is with you, O valiant warrior.' Then Gideon said to him, 'O my lord, if the Lord is with us, why then has all this happened to us? And where are all His miracles which our fathers told us about, saying "Did not the Lord bring us up from Egypt?" **But now the Lord has abandoned us** *and given us into the hand of Midian. And the Lord looked at him and said, 'Go in this your strength and deliver Israel from the hand of Midian. Have I not sent you?' And he said to Him, 'O Lord, how shall I deliver Israel? Behold, my family is the least in Manasseh, and I am the youngest in my father's house.' But the Lord said to him, 'Surely I will be with you, and you shall defeat Midian as one man.' So Gideon said to Him, 'If now I have found favor in Thy sight, then show me a sign that it is Thou who speakest with me.'" ... When Gideon saw that he was the angel of the Lord, he said, 'Alas, O Lord God! For now I have seen the angel of the Lord face to face.' And the Lord said to him, 'Peace to you, do not fear; you shall not die.' Then Gideon built an altar there to the Lord and named it The Lord is Peace. To this day it is still in Ophrah of the Abiezrites" (Judges 6:11-17, 22-24).*

At this time the Midianites had been greatly oppressing Israel. Gideon felt like a nobody. He could see no hope of success or victory. When the angel arrived, Gideon was simply trying to survive by hiding from the enemy in the wine press. The angel immediately addressed Gideon in the way that God saw him. As a valiant warrior. (Gideon's behavior was not, at the present time, that of a valiant warrior).

Gideon felt certain that God didn't love him. If He did, why would He allow such calamity to come upon Israel? (v.13) Gideon was full of fear of death, physical as well as soulish. Looking totally to himself to meet his own needs, Gideon's eyes were focused on himself, in self-pity. He said, "Even if God did love me, and were with me, I'm a nobody. I can't do anything. My family is from a very unimportant tribe in Israel. Not only that, but my family is despised and looked down upon even within our own tribe. Not only that, but I am the youngest and least important in my worthless, unimportant family. If you want a deliverer for Israel, look to a better man, from a better family, from a better tribe. I'm totally unworthy and incapable. *I'm a nothing.*"

At first, Gideon did not realize that an angel of the Lord was speaking to him. When he discovered the truth, in verse 22, Gideon became convinced that he was going to die. The Lord was able to finally lift Gideon out of his deception and false plumb line images through constantly speaking the word of truth to him. The angel kept insisting, "God does favor you. He is with you. You are a valiant warrior. You are valuable and important. God will use you."

We can see how the fear within Gideon was created by the negative circumstances, false plumb line images, and lies about God and himself that Gideon believed. Fear motivated him to walk in pride as he focused on himself in self-pity, unworthiness, and rebellion. When the Lord came to Gideon and revealed His will for Gideon's life, he rebelled against God and opposed Him and His will.

Motivated by fear, Gideon originally decided to put his faith in false plumb line images rather then in the truth God had spoken. This was the poisoning of the serpent in the wall. Praise God! Gideon was set free as he heard the Word of the Lord, finally put faith in that Word and in God, and came into the experience of the truth of who God said he was, instead of who he had previously believed and experienced himself to be.

Chapter Ten:
The Fourth Mode
Of Fleshly Operation

The fourth mode through which a Christian can walk in the flesh is characterized by the person feeling like a somebody, but having no hope of victory or success in his life. This has occurred as he has become convinced, through wrong interpretation of words and experiences, that he will always be defeated by forces outside of his control and greater than himself. This fourth mode of flesh is characterized as follows:

Experience of Fear		Experience of Self
Identity	Welfare	Plumb Line
No Value	Needs Not Met	Self-Image
1. Unconscious	Conscious	Somebody
		no hope-defeat-loser

When walking in this mode of flesh, a Christian believes: "I'm a somebody and am important and of value. I deserve to be treated fairly and justly. However, I'm not being treated fairly and am constantly being cheated and robbed. I'm not in victory now, and won't ever be, because others (perhaps God) are against me and I can't win. It's unfair, and I'm doomed to this life of defeat. Therefore, if 'they' (God, or whoever) won't play the game fairly, then I won't play in their game."

The "they" in this mode of thinking can be God, parents, employer, spouse or anyone with whom this person has a relationship. Things have not gone as well as this person would like, so he blames God and others for his negative circumstances. He trusts in himself and his own abilities, and he believes that he has done every reasonable thing required to bring about God's blessing and prosperity in his life. However, because this has not worked, and blessing hasn't come, the Christian blames God for being unfair and unjust in His dealings.

Let's call this person, "Richard." Richard, like those in all the other modes of flesh, doubts God's love for him and believes that love, honor, and esteem are rewarded on a performance basis. He believes that he has performed more than adequately, and that he is righteous and deserving of love, honor, and esteem from God and others. Because he is *doing* everything possible to gain victory, and his circumstances haven't improved, Richard is frustrated and angry inside.

Great fear of death is produced in Richard because he feels at the mercy of forces over which he has no control. They are "much more powerful" than he is. Richard thinks that even prayer, confessing the Word and the name of Jesus don't seem to help. Therefore, intense pride and rebellion operate through Richard in order to deal with the fear. He lives in great self-righteousness and trusts in his own reasoning and abilities. He is convinced that he is right, and is doing everything he is supposed to be doing. It should work — but it isn't working. The result? More fear is produced, because pride is not working, and Richard is unable to exalt himself above the circumstances. He enters into rebellion against whomever or whatever he blames for his negative situation, and this rebellion is usually open. He will directly oppose or flee from any person or circumstance that he believes is creating the death in his life.

Richard's perception of God is that of a powerful authority who is unjust and doesn't treat him fairly. God can't be pleased. It's not possible to win His favor and blessing. Richard observes God blessing others who are far less righteous and obedient, but God never blesses him. Richard believes that God is really the source of the problems and negative circumstances in his life. To him, this is very unfair. Inside, he is quite frustrated and angry with God.

Richard's flesh motivates him to view himself as righteous and worthy of value and esteem. He believes that he is of value because of his status and performance. He believes that he is righteous in and of himself because of his obedience and good works. Every time that Richard works hard toward a good and right goal, some other person, or God Himself, (so he thinks) seems to jerk the rug out from under him to keep him from realizing the fruit and accomplishment of the goal. He doesn't realize that the true source of his calamity is the poisonous serpent dwelling inside his own heart.

As Richard walks in rebellion against God and others, he justifies his attitude of pride through self-righteousness. Perceiving other people around him in much the same way he perceives God, Richard feels that those with whom he is in relationship also treat him unfairly and without due respect and honor. He always seems to be cheated and robbed by others. Because he is in pride and self righteousness, Richard often uses the Word of God as law in the lives of others close to him. (And the law always brings death.) Those to whom he does this also then tend to shy away from him to avoid the emotional death of the law. Richard, blinded to his own pride, believes that he has just been ministering the Word of God. If another person dislikes and rejects him for doing so, then Richard is "suffering and being persecuted for the sake of Christ and the gospel." The truth is that he is suffering for the sake of his own flesh.

Because his needs are not met and he is in great fear, Richard often places substantial demands of commitment, love, and honor on those to whom he is close. This puts others around him in fear, for they cannot meet his needs sufficiently. They back away from him. Then, because Richard fails to see his pride and rebellion, he interprets this as unfair treatment and cruel rejection.

Because he judges those who reject him, Richard grows to expect most people to reject him. Unless another person is walking in the spirit, sure enough, Richard is able to draw rejection right out of them. Whenever someone ministers the truth to a person walking in this fourth mode, that he is walking in the flesh in pride and rebellion, he may deny it, justify himself, and regard them as "one more person who doesn't understand." Another option is that Richard may truly see the truth and agree with it, but switch manifestations of pride and rebellion, resulting in guilt, condemnation, and self-pity. He may say, "You are right. It's all my own fault, and I'll never be any good. All I do is hurt others and myself. I am sure that God has given up on me a long time ago, and that is why nothing ever works for me."

The best scriptural example of a person walking in the flesh in this fourth mode is Job during his affliction. Remember that, before his affliction, Job was walking in the second mode of flesh. Due to the experience of affliction and fear of physical death (physical, material, relational, and soulical) Job switched to the fourth mode of greater outward pride and open rebellion.

*"Oh that **my vexation were actually weighed, and laid in the balances together with my iniquity!** For then it would be heavier than the sand of the seas, Therefore my words have been rash. For the arrows of the Almighty are within me; Their poison my spirit drinks; The **terrors of God** are arrayed against ... But it is still my consolation, And I rejoice in unsparing pain, That I have not denied the words of the Holy One"* (Job 6:2-4,10).

Job believed the lie that God was afflicting him. In verse 2, he revealed his belief that God's blessing or wrath came according to his performance. In verse 10, Job speaks in self-righteousness that he has not denied God, even though God has afflicted him (so he thinks).

*"Though I am righteous, my mouth will condemn me; **Though I am guiltless, He will declare me guilty.** I am guiltless; therefore I say, '**He destroys the guiltless and the wicked.'** If the scourge kills suddenly, He mocks the despair of the innocent"* (Job 9:20-23).

Here, Job once again declares his righteousness and God's unfair treatment. God condemns the guiltless and mocks the despair of the innocent, according to Job:

"For He is not a man as I am that I may answer Him, That we may go to court together. There is no umpire between us, who may lay his hand upon us both. Let Him remove His rod from me, and let not dread of Him terrify me. Then I would speak and not fear Him; But I am not like that in myself ... "But I would speak to the Almighty. And I desire to argue with God" (Job 9:32-35; 13:3).

Since God is God, Job can't argue with Him. Job says, "God is arbitrary and unjust." Because God is unjust, Job believes he has reason to argue and rebel.

"Then Job responded, 'Truly then you are the people, And with you wisdom will die! But I have intelligence as well as you; I am not inferior to you. And who does not know such things as these? I am a joke to my friends. The one who called on God, and He answered him; The just and blameless man is a joke'" (Job 12:1-4).

Job tells his counselors, "I am just as intelligent as you; don't try to counsel me."

"Be silent before me so that I may speak; Then let come on me what may. Why should I take my flesh in my teeth, and put my life in my hands: Though He slay me, I will hope in Him. Nevertheless I will argue my ways before Him. This also will be my salvation, For a godless man may not come before His presence. Listen carefully to my speech, and let my declaration fill your ears. Behold now, I have prepared my case; I know that I will be vindicated. Who will contend with me? For then I would be silent and die... How many are my iniquities and sins? Make known to me my rebellion and my sin" (Job 13:13-19,23).

Here Job uses the manipulative technique of "false openness and humility." "Though He slay me, yet will I serve Him." How righteous and pious! These words sound so good. Job must have thought he was really spiritual to say such a thing. In verse 23, Job said, "Lord, if I'm in sin or rebellion, show me." But I believe that he was really thinking this addendum: "But I'm sure that I'm not. I'm right, and God will have to realize it soon."

*"Know then that **God has wronged me**, And has closed His net around me. Behold, I cry, 'Violence!' But I get no answer; I shout for help, but there is no justice ... **Pity me, pity me, O you my friends**, For the hand of God has struck me" (Job 19:6-7;21). "Then these three men ceased answering Job, because he was righteous in his own eyes. But the anger of Elihu, the son of Barachel the Buzite, of the family of Ram burned; against Job his anger burned, **because he justified himself before God"** (Job 32:1,2).*

During this time, poor Job was deceived (by the serpent in his heart) into believing that he truly was right, and that God was wrong and unjust. The truth was that Satan, not God, was afflicting Job. Through deception and the false plumb line images that were already present in Job, Satan was then able to convince Job that God was the enemy, not the refuge. The only one who truly had power to deliver Job was the very one of whom Job was afraid. Job certainly doubted God's love for him and believed that God did not have his best interest and welfare at heart. Fear in Job was very intense, and, thus, pride and rebellion were also intense.

Job desperately needed to go to God, trust in His love, repent of unbelief, fear, pride and rebellion, and receive God's forgiveness. Obviously, we have a far more effective convenant with God today and far greater power and authority over the devil, through the blood of Jesus, than Job. But Job still did not walk in the power that was available to him at that time. Consequently, he was cut off from the *zoe* life of God by pride and rebellion due to the ignorance that comes from hardness of heart (Ephesians 4:18). We, like Job, need to know that our battle in life is not against God, but against sin in our flesh that has deceived us, and against the devil and demonic spirits. Now look at another scriptural example of a person walking in the fourth mode of flesh.

"Now Samuel was dead, and all Israel had lamented him and buried him in Ramah, his own city. And Saul had removed from the land those who were mediums and spiritists. So the Philistines

gathered together and came and camped in Shunem; and Saul gathered all Israel together and they camped in Gilboa. When Saul saw the camp of the Philistines, **he was afraid and his heart trembled greatly.** When Saul inquired of the Lord, **the Lord did not answer him,** either by dreams or by Urim or by prophets. Then Saul said to his servants, '**Seek for me a woman who is a medium,** that I may go to her and inquire of her.' And his servants said to him, 'Behold, there is a woman who is a medium at Endor.' Then Saul disguised himself by putting on other clothes, and went, he and two men with him, and they came to the woman by night; and he said, 'Conjure up for me please, and bring for me whom I shall name to you.' But the woman said to him, 'Behold, you know what Saul has done, how he has cut off those who are mediums and spiritists from the land. Why are you then laying a snare for my life to bring about my death?' And Saul vowed to her by the Lord, saying, 'As the Lord lives, there shall be no punishment come upon you for this thing.' Then the woman said, 'Whom shall I bring up for you?' And he said, 'Bring up Samuel for me.' When the woman saw Samuel, she cried out with a loud voice; and the woman spoke to Saul, saying, 'Why have you deceived me? For you are Saul.' And the king said to her, 'Do not be afraid; but what do you see?' And the woman said to Saul, 'I see a divine being coming up out of the earth.' And he said to her, 'What is his form?' And she said, 'An old man is coming up, and he is wrapped with a robe.' And Saul knew that it was Samuel, and he bowed with his face to the ground and did homage. Then Samuel said to Saul, 'Why have you disturbed me by bringing me up?' And Saul answered, 'I am greatly distressed; for the Philistines are waging war against me, and God has departed from me and answers me no more, either through prophets or by dreams; therefore, I have called you, that you may make known to me what I should do.' And Samuel said, 'Why, then, do you ask me, since the Lord has departed from you and become your adversary? And the Lord has done accordingly as He spoke through me; for the Lord has torn the kingdom out of your hand and given it to your neighbor, to David' " (I Samuel 28:3-17).

When a person is operating in the flesh in any mode, they cannot hear from God or receive revelation in the spirit, but they always believe God has departed from them, not that they have departed from God. This is due to deception. Saul had been unable to hear from the Lord for several years. He never really did understand why this had happened. The intensity of fear operating through Saul had increased over the years, and in this chapter, we find Saul experiencing tremendous fear of actual physical death. Consequently, Saul was motivated by sin in his flesh to move in great pride and rebellion.

When Saul was unable to hear from the Lord, instead of asking God to reveal where he was walking in the flesh and what was the blockage preventing him from fellowshiping with the Lord, Saul devised his own plan (motivated by fear, pride and rebellion) to discover God's will. He decided to engage a spirit medium to conjure the prophet, Samuel, back from the dead.

Saul had no trust in God. His trust had been totally in men, Samuel, and himself. Because God wouldn't answer him directly, Saul was no doubt angry, bitter, and frustrated with God. In fact, Saul felt completely justified in doing what God had expressly forbidden, because God "wouldn't help" him. Saul probably thought, "God isn't helping me. He won't even reveal His will to me. I have prayed. I have fasted. I've sought Him day and night. I've done everything possible, and yet God is silent. If I don't get some direction, we'll all be destroyed by the Philistines."

God had spoken to Israel's past leaders, and even to Saul. When God became silent, Saul thought, "God just wants to let His people perish. This whole situation is His fault. If He appointed me as king over Israel, why won't He give me direction for the nation? If only Samuel were still alive! Maybe a medium could raise him from death to tell me what to do." Because of Saul's great fear, he applied natural wisdom for a plan to obtain guidance. Yet this plan entailed doing exactly that which God had expressly forbidden! In rebellion, Saul engaged a spirit medium to bring Samuel back from the dead and, in doing so, used the James 3:15 type of wisdom which is not from above, but is earthly, unspiritual and even demonic. Saul was in total defiance against the truth.

Fear of death always ends by producing in a person the very thing of which he was afraid. Through Saul's rebellion against God, the result was only more fear. Saul never did repent, and he ultimately lost his physical life in battle with the Philistines the following day. The sad part is that Saul undoubtedly felt that he was doomed to failure and defeat by God. God had departed from Saul and hadn't spoken to him for several years, so he felt he was just an "innocent victim" in God's plan to give the kingdom to David. It was just Saul's "destiny" to die at the hands of the Philistines. This is the type of reasoning produced by the fourth mode of flesh. In truth, Saul could have received revelation of sin from God, repented, run to God (not away from Him in rebellion) and received life and peace at anytime. The Christian operating in this fourth mode may not outwardly or knowingly direct his rebellion toward God. He does walk in rebellion toward God, but he may do so entirely through deception. He may think, "I'm serving God and being obedient to Him," but be carrying out a God-inspired plan in the flesh, in rebellion against God.

Years ago, a couple came to my office for marital counseling. Both partners were walking almost totally in the flesh in their relationship toward one another. George was walking according to the fourth mode and Linda, according to the third. George was so convinced that he was right and his wife wrong that he didn't feel the need for counseling. Consequently, they didn't come as a couple, but George would frequently call to make counseling appointments for his wife.

Both had been married more than once before and, of course, carried judgments and expectancies with them from their former marriages. Both parties were operating in a great deal of fear. Linda was aware of her fears, but George would not acknowledge fear operating through him. When they were first married, neither was walking closely with the Lord. However, through the course of their 11 years of marriage, George had grown a tremendous amount spiritually, but Linda not as much.

When I first met Linda and George, they were both believers. George, however, had far more spiritual knowledge than his wife and really considered himself to be far more spiritual than she. He was in the Word and prayer frequently, while she was not. George had been severely abused verbally in past marriages, which had badly damaged his self-image. Thus, he had not felt honored, esteemed, or valued in past relationships. Since he had entered into a closer relationship with the Lord, George had seen that he was of value and important to the Lord. He had taken the stance that he wasn't a doormat for other people to walk on. He was worthy of honor and esteem because God had made him such through Jesus, and he was to be the head of his household.

George believed that, in taking this attitude, he was trusting in the Lord and walking in a "good self-image". He previously had a "poor self-image" and knew that God wanted more for him. The truth was, however, that he wasn't trusting in the Lord or walking in the spirit. He was walking in the flesh and trusting in himself as having inherent value in his flesh. He was not trusting in Jesus. Unconsciously motivated by fear of death, fear of being put down, physically or verbally assaulted, and being hurt, George's flesh was reacting to this fear in both pride and rebellion. In order to avoid hurt from Linda, he was walking in great pride, exalting himself spiritually far above her. He felt extremely righteous, patient, and long-suffering to put up with her fear, anger, and lack of spirituality. If anyone ever tried to call attention to his pride, George saw this as a put-down designed to place him back into a "poor self-image." Consequently, he vehemently resisted.

This pride, of course, pushed Linda into more fear and made her back away from George all the more. Essentially, pride was motivating George to make cutting, sarcastic comments to her quite frequently. When Linda would withdraw from him or retaliate in anger or return another cutting remark, George believed she was trying to put him down again, and he *refused* to allow that! He believed he was being persecuted unjustly, "for righteousness sake." In this state of mind, George would call to make a counseling appointment for Linda so that she would stop treating him unfairly.

George, unknowingly, was not only reacting in pride, but was in great rebellion toward his wife, as well. Because he considered himself spiritual and Linda unspiritual, he didn't feel that her opinions or thoughts had any value. He was too "spiritual and humble" to admit this directly, but believed it subtly and conveyed it to her. Consequently, he operated independently of Linda and resisted her in most of her ideas and plans. He continued in strong involvement at church, in his study of the Word, and in encouraging his wife to go to counseling appointments. While operating almost entirely in natural wisdom and trusting in himself, George thought that he was in the spirit and trusting in God.

As they were nearing retirement age, George began to conceive of a business which he wanted them to pursue during their retirement. This business was in a field where George had considerable experience and expertise. He believed with all his heart that the Lord had given him the idea and plan. However, this business required the investment of a substantial amount of the money that they had saved over the years. As George shared this vision with his wife, he expected her to be as excited about it as he was. Unfortunately, Linda wasn't very excited about it at all. She feared they might lose all their money. Immediately, he assumed this was a typical reaction from Linda. After all, she "was always full of fear, was unspiritual, and couldn't really hear from the Lord." He was absolutely convinced God had called him to pursue this business vision, as it also entailed some aspects of ministry. George then told his wife he intended to pursue the business/ministry plan God had given him whether she chose to come along or not. He had to obey God above man. Even if she couldn't hear God and overcome her fear and lack of trust in God, George was going to have to obey the Lord's call. This statement, of course, served to only catapult Linda into greater fear. George believed that, in taking such a stand, he was trusting and obeying God. Willing to sacrifice his marriage in order to accomplish this vision, he told his wife, "You will not stand in the way of my obedience to God."

In fact, George was not trusting God at all. He was trusting in himself and his own natural wisdom to carry out a vision that, I believe, the Lord probably really did give him. Neither Linda's lack of spirituality or her own fear was causing her to resist him. Rather it was George's tremendous pride and rebellion toward her that put her in fear and motivated her to resist him. The serpent operating within had deceived George so that he was unable to receive revelation of this from God.

George, having been deceived, was walking in the flesh, primarily in the fourth mode. However, he was not blaming God outwardly for his situation. He was blaming his wife. In belief that he was obeying God by rebelling against his wife, he was using natural wisdom, walking in the flesh to accomplish his vision, and rebelling against God in the process, just as Saul once did.

To make matters more complicated, George had been "praying" with several of his Christian friends who had encouraged him in his position toward his wife. They said, "Yes, you can't deny the Lord for the sake of your wife." Thus, they had further justified his position from the Word:

"Yet if the unbelieving one leaves, let him leave; the brother or the sister is not under bondage in such cases, but God has called us to peace" (I Corinthians 7:15).

George and his Christian friends said that Linda was acting like an unbeliever. Since she was acting like an unbeliever, this scripture applied, and he was free to treat her as an unbelieving wife. His friends encouraged him to continue on in his "obedience" to the Lord regarding his pursuit of business/ministry plans, regardless of his wife. If she chose to "quit being obstinate and rebellious" and come with him, fine. But if she continued to act like an unbeliever, resist him and back away from him, then he was no longer under obligation to her as her husband. Or, if she chose to leave him, then let her go.

God's purposes in George's life were to reveal how he had been deceived and had related to his wife from pride and rebellion. He could then repent, allow his mind to begin to be renewed, and walk in the spirit with his wife. This would then help to set her free from the fear that she had been walking in so that she could hear from the Lord. God desired the two of them to find unity regarding what they were to do.

In actuality, the marriage relationship was of much higher priority to the Lord than the fulfillment of George's business/ministry plans. God wanted George to see how his flesh was governing his soul and destroying his marriage so that he could repent and walk in the spirit in his relationship with his wife. Then, in unity, they could fulfill a business/ministry vision. However, by bowing his neck and bulldozing over the top of his wife in rebellion, George was also rebelling against God. The Lord may have given him the vision, but by trying to accomplish it in the flesh, he was in rebellion against God and missing His top priority for his life.

Not realizing it, George was moving in the flesh, just as Moses did when he killed the Egyptian and attempted to exalt himself as leader over the Israelites to deliver them from Egypt (Exodus 2:11-14). He had received the correct vision from the Lord to lead the Israelites out of bondage from Egypt. But when Moses tried to fulfill that vision in the flesh, he ended up having to flee Egypt for his life and spend 40 years in the wilderness tending sheep before the vision could come to pass.

George, motivated by the intense fear within him, felt that he had to put Linda down. He felt that his vision wouldn't come to pass unless he forced it to happen. He was terribly frustrated, because Linda wouldn't change, and it seemed that their situation was only getting worse. The serpent (sin in his flesh) had so poisoned his soul that he could only blame his wife for their difficulties and wasn't open to allow the Lord to give him revelation of sin. He only saw his wife as a lion or bear. He didn't see the serpent hiding in the wall of his own heart.

I am not making a statement here about headship within a family. There are many other books dealing with that topic. You may ask, "Aren't there some issues that are so important (perhaps moral issues) that if you can't come to agreement, it is necessary to break unity or relationship within a marriage?" I agree that there are rare times when this may be necessary. However, before a marriage partner does so, he had better diligently seek the Lord regarding how his own flesh may be the cause of the partners' disagreement and negative reaction, and be willing to repent of any sin which God may reveal.

Before a husband or wife breaks unity with their marriage partner over an unresolved issue, they had better be certain that it is truly a matter of conscience and unresolvable and not a simple result of their own walking in the flesh. Otherwise they will think they are being obedient to God and being persecuted for righteousness sake, when they are in reality only experiencing the natural consequences of the law of sin and death.

The last time I saw George and Linda, Linda was becoming slightly more favorable toward George's business/ministry plan. However, George still had not been open to receive revelation from God, of fear, pride or rebellion, and consequently, was still walking in the flesh in most areas of his life.

So we see that Christians operating in any mode of flesh can easily walk in rebellion against God through fleshly endeavors to obey God. Because they are not trusting God and receiving His direction clearly, they will often attempt to carry out godly plans using natural wisdom and fleshly motives, thus resulting ultimately in failure and frustration.

Chapter Eleven:
Freedom Through
Walking In The Spirit

*"But I say, walk by the spirit, and you **will not** carry out the desire of the flesh. For the flesh sets its desire against the spirit, and the spirit against the flesh; for these are in opposition to one another, so that you may not do the things that you please"* (Galatians 5:16-17).

If we walk in the spirit, our minds, wills and emotions will be directed by our born-again spirits. It is then impossible to be motivated by our flesh. The last five chapters have outlined sin in our flesh as being very deceptive, a powerful, unconscious, motivating factor in our lives. However, it is more important to remember that the nature of Jesus in our spirits is far more powerful than sin in our flesh. In truth, sin in our flesh has no power except that which we allow it through deception.

So, according to Galatians 5:16-17, the path to freedom is not in striving against sin in our flesh, but to walk in the spirit. Our attempts are not channeled toward an avoidance of walking in the flesh. Rather, follow the leading of the Spirit. If you try to avoid walking in the flesh, you will be inevitably drawn into using the Word as a law in your mind, and you will lose your battle.

Our only identification should be with the truth of who we are in Jesus Christ in our spirit. Doing so will prevent the otherwise endless shifts from one mode of walking in the flesh to another without dealing with the root false plumb line images and fear.

Galatians 5 lists many manifestations of the flesh and labels them as "deeds of the flesh." These include: idolatry, lust, hatred, jealousy, murder, adultery, greed, bitterness, stealing, slander, strife, sorcery. These deeds, of course, emanate from sin in our flesh which captures our soul. I believe that each one of these manifestations is ultimately rooted in either pride, rebellion, or both. Each one stems from the desire to exalt oneself above other people (pride) or to meet one's goals or needs independent from God (rebellion).

These deeds of the flesh manifest in us only when our flesh is governing our soul and we are not abiding in the love of God. Therefore, the ultimate solution for any of these manifestations is to receive revelation of our false plumb line images based on the doubt of God's love. This image can only produce fear — fear motivates us to not trust God or abide in His love. Love — God's love — is our key to entering the fullness of His life in the Spirit:

> *"We know that we have passed out of death into life, because we love the brethren. He who does not love abides in death" (John 3:14).*

At the new birth, our spirits passed from death into life. Now our souls must enter this life by walking in the spirit. You may ask the question, "How, then, do I really walk in the spirit? I don't want to just move from one mode of walking in the flesh to another. How can I be free from deception to walk in the spirit?"

If you are honestly asking this question, then you have already taken the first step toward freedom. The first step is to realize that much of the time when you thought that you already were walking in the spirit, you were in fact deceived into walking in the flesh. The simple revelation *that* you have been deceived by sin in your flesh allows you to open yourself up before God to allow revelation of the extent of that deception. Now He can begin to set you free from deception to walk in the spirit.

The Lord has revealed seven major steps that have helped me to walk in the spirit and not in the flesh. These steps are not a magic formula for walking in the spirit.

Walking in the spirit is what allows your soul to be directed and dominated by the Holy Spirit *through your spirit*. This creates a vital, dynamic relationship with the living person of Jesus Christ. Therefore, no "seven-step formula" will in itself free you from bondage to your flesh. Only the power of Jesus Christ activated by your faith in Him can free you. I have felt led by the Lord to share these seven steps with you only as motivation for you to put your faith in the living God who loves you and longs to give you revelation, set you free, impart to you His *zoe* life, and make you successful in Him.

As you read through the rest of this chapter, please remember that principles and understanding alone will not break the yoke of bondage in your soul. The anointing of God coming through His Word is what breaks the yoke of bondage (Isaiah 10:27). Allow God to give you personal revelation in your spirit and then be obedient to the Lord.

STEP ONE: Allow Conviction

"I now rejoice, not that you were made sorrowful, but that you were made sorrowful to the point of repentance; for you were made sorrowful according to the Will of God, in order that you might not suffer loss in anything through us. For the sorrow that is according to the will of God produces a repentance without regret, leading to salvation; but the sorrow of the world produces death" (2 Corinthians 7:9-10).

Once you have discovered yourself to be walking in the flesh in certain areas of your life, allow God to convict you of the sin. Attempts to repent without conviction of sin do no good. Without conviction of sin, repentance will not bring *zoe* life and freedom into your soul.

Nine or ten months before we were ministering in Poland, Jean had attempted to minister to me about the pride in which I was walking. I thought about this and prayed about it. But I didn't really believe that it was true. I finally concluded, "If Jean sees it, it must really be true." So I prayed and repented of pride and asked the Lord's forgiveness.

The point is, because I had never really received revelation from the Lord of sin and didn't feel convicted of it, I wasn't set free. I remained in the same deception as I had been in previously. Only later, with Jean in Poland, did I really open myself up to the Lord, allow Him to reveal the deception, and experience conviction of sin.

Conviction of sin comes when you open up to the Lord and ask Him honestly to reveal the sin in your flesh that has captured your soul. Remember that it is not you who is sinning. It is the sin in your flesh that has captured your soul (Romans 7:17-20). As you open yourself up to the Lord, allow Him to convict you of the superficial deeds and the deeper false plumb line images of sin. Let Him convict you of lust, anger, hatred, jealousy, adultery, greed, drunkenness, bitterness, stealing, slander, quarreling, etc. Let Him show you judgments, manipulation and false expectancies. Then ask the Lord to show you the pride and rebellion which have been operating through you. Ask God to convict you of any fears of being unimportant and having no value to Him or others. Allow conviction of the fear that God isn't faithful and won't meet your needs. Let Him convict you of trusting in yourself and believing God's love is dependent on your performance. The Lord will reveal any mistrust of His love. This is all sin of which you need to be convicted.

Before you open yourself up to the Lord in such a way and ask Him to bring conviction of sin, it is very important to bind Satan and demonic spirits from speaking to you. You can do this by simply commanding them in the name of Jesus to be silent. Their purpose is to bring condemnation and worldly sorrow, and these result in soulish death, not repentance and life. If you feel condemnation and judgment, these are not from God. God loves you and never condemns you! (Romans 8:1).

As you come to your Father with an honest heart,

asking Him to convict you of sin, He will give you deep revelation in the spirit of sin that has been operating through you. Such true conviction of sin will automatically lead you to the second step.

STEP TWO: Repent of Sin

"And your ears will hear a word behind you, 'This is the way, walk in it,' whenever you turn to the right or left. And you will defile your graven images, overlaid with silver, and your molten images plated with gold. You will scatter them as an impure thing; and say to them, 'Be gone!' Then He will give you rain for the seed which you will sow in the ground, and it will be rich and plenteous; on that day your livestock will graze in a roomy pasture" (Isaiah 30:21-23). "For though we walk in the flesh, we do not war according to the flesh. For the weapons of our warfare are not of the flesh, but divinely powerful for the destruction of fortresses. We are destroying speculations and every lofty thing raised up against the knowledge of God, and we are taking every thought captive to the obedience of Christ" (2 Corinthians 10:3-5).

After God has convicted us of sin, godly sorrow leads us to repentance. We then address the graven images in which we have walked and renounce them. Say to those false plumb line images, even as Isaiah spoke, *"Be gone!"* (Isaiah 30:22).

Repentance means to "turn away from," "renounce," and to "die to sin in your flesh." You need to repent of all that of which God has convicted you on every level. Ultimately, you need to repent of placing faith and trust in the false plumb line images. These are graven images that need to be cast down.

The basic false plumb line images are lies which, in your mind, have become strongholds and fortresses. You have experienced these images for most of your life. It may seem as though a part of you is being torn out of your life. And, in a sense, that is true. But the part that is being torn out is malignant — cancerous — and has been poisoning and destroying you. It is not truly you. You are truly who Jesus has recreated you to be in the spirit.

The identity that you have perceived through false plumb line images is one that you must now totally relinquish, renounce, and allow to die. It is a false identity based on lies. Your true identity is in Jesus Christ *in your spirit.*

As stated in 2 Corinthians 10:4, tear down these strongholds and fortresses. Repent of the false images, fear, pride and rebellion. You might pray something like the following, "I renounce the lie of belief that God doesn't love me, isn't faithful to me, and won't take care of me. Father, I confess that I believed these lies about You and about myself. I now realize that they are lies. I repent of believing them. I ask you to forgive me and cleanse me by the blood of Jesus."

Perhaps, while you have been praying, various experiences from the past have entered your mind. Perhaps these are experiences that helped to create or reinforce one or more of the false plumb line images. I have found that the Holy Spirit will bring these experiences to our remembrance so that we can repent of wrong interpretations of the circumstances.

If the Lord has brought such experiences to your remembrance, seize your opportunity to repent of those wrong interpretations and responses. This is an important part of allowing the Lord to renew your mind to the truth of who God is and who you are. Finally, remember that if God does not bring experiences to mind, don't "work them up." Let the Holy Spirit do the work.

Perhaps the Lord has also reminded you of various people who have hurt you in the past, or may be hurting you now. Now is the time to forgive them! Forgiveness means to "hold accountable no longer." Release them. Let them go. Consider them as if they had not offended you. Only the deception of sin in your flesh would try to convince you that you are justified in holding bitterness against someone. Repent of that resentment and bitterness, because it is part of a stronghold in your soul. Tear it down. Say to it "Be gone!"

Repentance is a tremendously powerful tool for healing and renewal by the hands of the Lord. However, by itself, repentance is insufficient to bring about freedom in the spirit within us. Thus, we must move on to the next step.

STEP THREE: *View in the Spirit*

"Therefore from now on we recognize no man according to the flesh; even though we have known Christ according to the flesh, yet now we know Him thus no longer" (2 Corinthians 5:16)."We are destroying speculations and every lofty thing raised up against the knowledge of God, and we are taking every thought captive to the obedience of Christ" (2 Corinthians 10:5).

Purpose to view yourself in the spirit. Don't identify with your flesh any longer. Take every thought of yourself captive to the obedience of Christ.

We saw earlier that like a camera, the soul creates the image of its focus. You then proceed to experience yourself through those false images. Now that you have repented of those images, it is necessary to create a new, true self-image in your soul. This image is based on the truth of who you are in your spirit. This is your focus.

If you find yourself experiencing continued sin in your life, don't receive it as "me." It is not you. It is sin in your flesh. Repent immediately and don't view yourself in the flesh.

By the way, don't view anyone else in the flesh either. View every other person as Jesus views them. (Even those who may be hurting you.) Allow the love of Jesus Christ to flow through your spirit into your soul and out to others. This is the mechanism by which others are healed and enter into right relationship with God.

STEP FOUR: *Receive the Truth*

"Therefore if any man is in Christ, he is a new creature; the old things passed away behold, new things have come" (2 Corinthians 5:17). "For you have been born again not of seed which is perishable but imperishable, that is, through the living and abiding word of God" (1 Peter 1:23). "And ye shall know the truth, and the truth shall make you free" (1 John 8:32).

A) *Receive the truth of who you are in Jesus Christ.* Acknowledge who you are in the spirit. Begin to place your trust and faith in God's Word about you — not in the way that you formerly experienced yourself, in what your emotions say, or in what anyone else says.

B) *Receive the truth of who God really is.* Now is the time to reach out to your Father in heaven who loves you and receive His unconditional love. The doubt of His love is what allowed false images to arise. Receipt of His perfect love is what casts them down. You are now free to truly receive God's limitless love for you. Allow Him to replace the old false image of Him in your soul with the true image of Himself.

In the future, whenever you have an experience that confirms an old false image of yourself or of God, don't receive it that way. Go to the Lord first, and ask for revelation. Don't interpret future words and experiences with your own natural mind. Go to the Lord first and ask Him for truth regarding who He is and what He is doing in your circumstance. If a circumstance appears to contradict God's truth, ask Him for wisdom and truth. Knowledge of the truth will guard you from slipping back into harmful self-images and false images of God.

STEP FIVE: Place Faith in the Blood of Jesus

"Being justified freely by His grace, through the redemption that is in Christ Jesus; Whom God hath set forth to be a propitiation, through faith in his blood, to declare His righteousness for the remission of sins that are past, through the forbearance of God" (Romans 3:24-25, KJV). *"But if we walk in the light as He Himself is in the light, we have fellowship with one another, and the blood of Jesus His Son cleanses us from all sin"* (I John 1:7).

Place faith in the cleansing power of the blood of Jesus Christ. God promises that the blood of Jesus cleanses you from *all* sin! Receive His cleansing power. John 1:7 doesn't say "has cleansed." It says "cleanses." Right now! The blood of Jesus is availing and effectual to cleanse you from all sin right now. Romans 3:25 says that you activate the cleansing power of the blood of Jesus by faith. Simply trust God! Believe that He is faithful and that the blood of Jesus will cleanse you now.

As you place your faith in the blood of Jesus, you can receive forgiveness, cleansing and purging in your soul from sin that once captured you. The blood of Jesus literally cleanses and purifies your soulish realm and heals your physical body as you receive the *zoe* life of God through your spirit.

John 1:1 tells us that in the beginning was the Word, and the Word was with God, *and the Word was God*. John 1:14 tells us that the Word became flesh. We know that this Word made flesh is Jesus Christ. Leviticus 17:11 reveals "the life of the flesh is in the blood" and that "it is the blood by reason of the life that makes atonement." John 1:4 says that "in Him (that is Jesus) was life *(zoe)*; and the life *(zoe)* was the light of men."

Since the life of the flesh is in the blood, the life *(zoe)* of the Word made flesh (Jesus) is in His blood. Since the life *(zoe)* in Him is the light of men, the blood which is the life *(zoe)* is the light of men.

Jesus said in John 6:63 "It is the spirit who gives life *(zoe),* the flesh profits nothing; the words that I have spoken to you are spirit and are life *(zoe).*" So if we receive Jesus' words, we receive life *(zoe)* which is also His blood, which is also the light of men.

When we receive the *zoe* life of God through walking in the spirit, receiving His Word, and placing faith in Jesus, our souls and bodies receive the blood of Jesus to purge, cleanse, heal, and deliver.

Place your trust in God and the blood of Jesus. By doing so, you receive the *zoe* of life of God in your soul. You are nullifying the law of sin and death in your life, and are activating the law of the spirit of life in Jesus.

STEP SIX: Walk in the Light

"But if we walk in the light as He Himself is in the light, we have fellowship with one another, and the blood of Jesus His Son cleanses us from all sin. If we say that we have no sin, we are

deceiving ourselves, and the truth is not in us. If we confess our sins, He is faithful and righteous to forgive us our sins and to cleanse us from all unrighteousness" (I John1:7-9).

We know from the above Scripture that the "light" is the Word — the life *(zoe)* and blood of Jesus. To abide in the Word, the *zoe* life, and the blood of Jesus, is to walk in His light. This is not a one-time experience, but a continual process.

It is the process by which our soul (James 1:21) and our mind are transformed (Romans 12:2). You can walk in the light constantly by repeating the previous five steps daily. I have noticed a process of transformation in my own life that occurs as I walk continually in the light.

When I first recognized my unconscious motivation to twist truths with Christy and Jan, I was convicted of lying. I was also convicted of fear, pride, rebellion, unbelief, trusting in self, and doubt of God's love. I repented of these sins, repented of regarding myself in the flesh, received the truth, placed my faith in the blood of Jesus, and began to walk in the light. After a short while, however, I caught some of the same manifestations of sin operating through me again. I immediately repented and received the truth again. This happened several times. Each time, I implemented the first five steps. Then, after a while, I noticed that I was beginning to become aware of sin even while it was still happening. Each time I repented and went through the other steps.

Not long afterward, I noticed that significant metamorphosis had already occurred: I began to catch my mind planning to twist the truth even before I had done it. I could then repent and come into truth even before I had yet acted upon a lie!

As I developed a habit of repenting from sin each time I caught it, I began to notice it earlier and earlier. I believe that this is the process of "renewing our mind" about which Paul spoke in Romans 12:2. Each time that I repented, my mind became a little more renewed to the truth.

Chapter 11 — Freedom in the Spirit

I described earlier these fleshly patterns of thought, emotions, and actions that establish themselves in the soul as deep-hardened grooves. Each time we walk in one of those patterns, we further deepen and harden a groove in our soul. However, each time we become aware of sin's motivation and repent, we soften and slowly erase those grooves. As the Holy Spirit continues to convict us, we repent and receive the truth and placing our trust in God, the grooves in our soul are incrementally diminished. Step by step, the grooves are filled in and remolded until they are finally eradicated. Hallelujah! New grooves are cut according to the truth of God.

Each time you repent, reject the lie and walk in the truth, you thus dispel death in your soul with the zoe life of God and allow the blood of Jesus to purge and cleanse your mind, will, and emotions.

Sometimes this recreation (in particular areas of our soul) is a process that takes some time. However, sometimes the anointing of God comes upon us so powerfully that the recreation of a particular area of our soul will occur instantaneously. I have seen it occur both ways. Don't be surprised or frustrated in either case. Simply be led by the Spirit of God and continue to walk in the light.

Once, a man whom I was counseling came in for his appointment feeling quite frustrated. He had dealt with a lifelong problem regarding his temper and had requested counseling primarily to deal with his frequent outbursts of anger. During counseling the week before, this man had repented of anger, fear, not trusting God, and not receiving God's love. Everything had gone fine for four or five days — but then, on the night before our session, he had blown up in anger and had said and done things for which he was very sorry.

When this man came back in for counseling he felt frustrated and defeated because he had believed that he was completely delivered from anger and his temper.

As I explained to him the process of the renewing of the mind and the transformation of the soul as he walked in the light, the man became hopeful. We prayed again, and he repented of sin and identifying and relating to himself in the old way.

This man had believed that he was an angry man. However, he was not angry in his spirit, but had simply yielded his soul to his flesh. Several weeks have now passed since that counseling session, and he has continued to view himself in the spirit rather than the flesh. Each time that anger has risen up, he has repented and found that where before he wasn't able to catch it until after it had seized him, he had begun catching the anger and repenting of it before it captured his soul. This man also found that anger rose up less and less frequently as he continued to identify himself in the spirit and walk in the light.

This is the process of crucifying the flesh and walking in the spirit that is described in James as the "trials and testing of our faith that produces endurance."

"Consider it all joy, my brethren, when you encounter various trials, Knowing that the testing of your faith produces endurance. And let endurance have its perfect result, that you may be perfect and complete, lacking in nothing" (James 1:2-4).

Remember, God works in your life through the law of the spirit of life (zoe) in Christ Jesus, not through the law of sin and death. Trials and testings are not due to God putting financial distress, mental or emotional torment, strife, calamity, destruction, or death upon you in order to test you.

Our own flesh is what causes us to encounter various trials and testings. Only through dying to our flesh, walking in the spirit, and exercising faith in God and His love for us can we become perfect and complete, *lacking in nothing*. If we walked in the spirit 100 percent of the time with perfect trust in God and in His love, we would have constant victory in every circumstance and situation. No matter how Satan, demonic spirits or other people attacked us, we would never experience death in our soul. We would always be flying in the law of the spirit of life in Jesus. We would always be victorious.

So I believe that the process of transforming the soul to the true spirit identity is what creates the trials and testing. The man who had been afflicted by anger was having his faith tested each time his flesh rose up in anger. As he each time, by the spirit, through repentance and faith, "crucified" his flesh (Romans 8:13), *zoe* life flooded his soul and gave him victory.

Two other aspects are critical. The first has to do with dwelling in God's Word daily. Jesus said His Words are spirit and life *(zoe)*. (John 6:63) We walk in the light by dwelling in the Word of God (the Bible). The *zoe* life of God, which is full of cleansing power, then enables our true spiritual identity to manifest in our souls. James 1:21 assures us that the engrafted Word is able to save (transform) your soul. As you read the Word daily and allow the Spirit of God to implant it into your soul, you will receive the *zoe* life of God.

It is imperative that you read and meditate in the Word of God every day. If you don't have a way in which God has led you to read and meditate in the Word, ask Him to reveal a way. There are many excellent study guides. But you must receive revelation from the Lord of how He wants you to meditate in His Word. It is absolutely essential that you spend a significant time in God's Word every day. You cannot afford not to.

The second most critical aspect of walking in the light is a commitment to daily prayer in the Holy Spirit:

"But you, beloved, building yourselves up on your most holy faith, praying in the Holy Spirit; keep yourselves in the love of God, waiting anxiously for the mercy of our Lord Jesus Christ to eternal life" (Jude 20-21). "For one who speaks in a tongue does not speak to men, but to God; for no one understands, but in his Spirit he speaks mysteries. But one who prophesies speaks to men for edification and exhortation and consolation. One who speaks in tongues edifies himself; but one who prophesies edifies the church" (I Corinthians 14:2-4).

The Word tells us that when we pray in the spirit we edify ourselves. We build ourselves up in faith. We are kept in the love of God. We are speaking to God. In our spirit, we are speaking mysteries. I believe that one of the mysteries we are speaking is expressed in Colossians 1:27 which is "Christ in you, the hope of glory."

When we pray in the spirit, our spirit prays and by-passes our natural mind (I Corinthians 14:14). The result is that our soul is edified and built up in faith.

The life of Jesus Christ in your spirit is released into your soul when you pray in the spirit. Christ in you, the hope of glory, who is already manifest in your spirit, becomes more manifest in your soul as you yield your tongue and voice to your spirit. This is something over which your flesh cannot gain control.

Your natural mind, dominated by your flesh, may try to tell you that you are not really praying in the spirit. "You are just making up the words." It can tell you that praying in the spirit is of no value. It will tell you every conceivable lie in order to stop you from praying in the spirit. This is because your carnal mind does not want you to yield your tongue and voice to the Spirit of God in your spirit. The edification and building up in the spirit is your key to a soul that is yielded more to the spirit rather than the flesh.

"And in the same way the spirit also helps our weakness; for we do not know how to pray as we should, but the Spirit Himself intercedes for us with groanings too deep for words: and He who searches the hearts knows what the mind of the Spirit is, because He intercedes for the saints according to the will of God" (Romans 8:26-27).

The Holy Spirit searches your heart (spirit and soul). He (the Holy Spirit) knows His plans regarding you. In other words, He knows God's will for you. And, Paul says, the Holy Spirit intercedes for you according to that perfect will. What might prevent you from walking in the fullness of God's will? The answer is your flesh. Verse 26 promises, however, that the Holy Spirit helps you in weakness or infirmity. This word translated, *weakness*, is the greek word *asthenia.*[1]

Vine's Expository Dictionary of Biblical Words defines this word as "an inability to produce results." So Verse 26 is saying that when you pray in the spirit, the Holy Spirit helps you overcome your human inability to produce results according to God's will.

Putting this all together then, it goes like this: The Holy Spirit knows the will of God for you in every area. Your flesh is the primary hindrance to your soul's true identity in Christ (already manifest in your spirit). This prevents you from knowing and walking in the will of God. The Holy Spirit then, knowing the will of God for you, searches your heart and discerns your inability to produce results because of your flesh. As you pray in the spirit, the Holy Spirit directs your spirit to pray perfect prayers according to God's will. The hindrances of your flesh are overcome and Christ in you, your hope of glory, is made manifest in your soul.

This is why Paul exhorts us that praying in the spirit is a critical offensive weapon that defeats the powers of darkness (Ephesian 6:17-18). As a matter of fact, Paul believed it to be so critical that he told the Ephesians to pray at *all times* in the spirit!

Paul linked praying in the spirit with the Word of God. I believe that praying in the spirit edifies and opens up the soul to receive the Word. After all, the engrafted Word saves your soul (James 1:21). Without revelation in the spirit from God through His Word, it cannot become engrafted or implanted. Praying in the spirit edifies our soul and makes it sensitive to the spirit so that it can receive revelation from God through the Word.

Years ago, I heard of a scientific study that correlated the growth of jungle vegetation with the sounds made by birds and other native animals. This study revealed that the vegetation grew far more prolifically in the presence of chirping birds and other animals than in isolation from such natural jungle sounds. Upon investigation, it was discovered that certain pitch and frequency sounds tend to cause the *stomata*, or pores of the leaves of the plants to open up. Upon opening, the pores were then able to receive nutrients that were naturally available in the jungle environment. Scientists discovered when similar vegetation was isolated from the natural sounds, although the same nutrients were available, pores of the plants failed to open sufficiently to receive the nutrients in the same degree and growth was far less noticeable.

In a similar way, I believe that praying in the spirit stimulates our soul to open up to our spirit. When we read the Word after praying in the spirit, our soul receives far greater revelation from God. In this way, the Word becomes engrafted and implanted within us.

I have proved this in my personal experience. I generally receive far more revelation from the Word when I first spend 45 minutes or more praying in the spirit. Establish a daily habit of prayer and meditation in the Word of God. This will help you to walk in the spirit.

I do not advocate you pray exclusively in the spirit. Paul exhorts us as follows:

"For if I pray in a tongue, my spirit prays, but my mind is unfruitful. What is the outcome then? I shall pray with the spirit and I shall pray with the mind also; I shall sing with the spirit and I shall sing with the mind also" (I Corinthians 14:14-15).

STEP SEVEN: Be Transformed

"And do not be conformed to this world, but be transformed by the renewing of your mind, that you may prove what the will of God is, that which is good and acceptable and perfect" (Romans 12:2). "Now the Lord is the Spirit; and where the Spirit of the Lord is, there is liberty. But we all, with unveiled face beholding as in a mirror the glory of the Lord, are being transformed into the same image from glory to glory, just as from the Lord, the Spirit" (2 Corinthians 3:17-18).

This step is not really a step that you take, but it is the final result of walking in the other six steps. As you allow God to convict you of the areas where you have walked in the flesh, and you continually repent, come into the truth and trust in God, the deep grooves of false images are naturally smoothed over and replaced with grooves according to the truth in the spirit. This is the process of renewing your mind.

Continue to identify with your spirit and not with your flesh, and the nature of Jesus Christ will manifest in your mind, will, and emotions. *This is true transformation!* You are not just changing from one mode of walking in the flesh to another. You are no longer motivated by fear. Rather, you are in the spirit and receiving God's unconditional love for you. As you do so, you are operating the Law of the Spirit of Life in Christ Jesus. Thus, you become totally free from the Law of Sin and Death. You begin to view your life according to the truth of your identity in Christ.

Romans 8:2

Law of the Spirit of Life In Christ Jesus
Receipt of God's Love

Message: You are unconditionally loved
and accepted in Christ! Your needs are met in Him

Faith

2 Corinthians 3:17-18
Life in the Spirit

Law of Sin and Death
Doubt of God's Love

Message: You are of no value,
worthless.

Message: God won't take care of
you. Your needs won't be met.

Fear

Identity			Welfare		
conscious nobody	unconscious somebody		conscious no hope-loser	unconscious hope-winner	
Pride	**Pride**		**Rebellion**	**Rebellion**	

1. **Allow God to convict you of sin.** (i.e., doubt of God's love, fear, pride, rebellion) (2 Cor. 7:9-10).
2. **Repent of sin** (Isaiah 30:21-23, 2 Cor. 10:3-5).
3. **Don't regard yourself after the flesh** (2 Cor. 5:16, 10:5).
4. **Acknowledge and receive the truth of who you are in Christ** (2 Cor. 5:17, 1 Peter 1:23, John 8:32).
5. **Place faith in the blood of Jesus and receive forgiveness and cleansing** (Rom. 3:25, 1 John 1:7).
6. **Walk in the light** (I John 1:7-9).
7. **Be transformed as your mind is renewed to the truth of God's love and faithfulness** (Rom. 12:2, 2 Cor. 3:17-18).

"But I say, walk by the spirit and you will not carry out the desire of the flesh" (Galatians 5:16-17).

Don't Miss These Tapes by Craig Hill

Please send the following:

☐ **HOW TO HEAR GOD'S VOICE** — Learn *specific steps* for receiving God's guidance in your life.
One tape — $5.00

☐ **AERODYNAMICS OF THE SPIRIT LIFE*** — Discover how to rise above the law of sin and death and operate from the law of life in Christ.
2-tape set — $10.00

☐ **PEACE VIA A WAR-TIME MENTALITY** — Learn how to destroy the works of the devil so that you can enjoy life in Christ.
2-tape set — $10.00

☐ **FREEDOM FROM FALSE IMAGES** — Discover how to exchange incorrect images of who you are for the image of Jesus Christ.
3-tape set — $15.00

☐ **HOW TO LIVE IN THE SPIRIT** — Learn how to live from your spirit that was recreated when you accepted Jesus, and transform your personality as a result — an in-depth teaching.
11-tape set — $45.00

*The 2-tape set, **AERODYNAMICS OF THE SPIRIT LIFE,** is part of the 11-tape set, **HOW TO LIVE IN THE SPIRIT.**

I am enclosing $_____

Name _____

Address _____

City State Zip _____

Telephone _____

Mail to: Craig S. Hill, **SPIRIT LIFE,** 7955 E. Arapahoe Court, Suite 3100, Englewood, Colorado 80112 (303) 773-2972.

"Receive with meekness the engrafted word, which is able to save your souls" (Jas. 1:21).

THE ENGRAFTED WORD, a newsletter edited by Craig S. Hill and Holly Smits, is complimentary and offers you:

- Teachings on how to live by the spirit
- A calendar of upcoming events

To receive your complimentary copy of THE ENGRAFTED WORD each month, please fill out the coupon below and mail to SPIRIT LIFE.

Spirit Life Seminars

SPIRIT LIFE, a ministry co-directed by Craig S. Hill, offers seminars based on the Word of God and led by the anointing of the Holy Spirit. We invite your church or community group to co-sponsor these seminars with us and look forward to hearing from you.

SPIRIT LIFE PRINCIPLES
Through this 25-30 hour seminar, you will: • Grow through the exciting life of walking in the spirit, not through experiencing the law of sin and death. • Be released from strongholds in your life—formerly known or unknown to you—that have kept you from experiencing God's best.

FOREVER FREE FROM EATING DISORDERS
By participating in this 20-hour seminar, you or your loved ones can be transfigured from eating disorders such as anorexia, bulimia, chronic overweight, binge eating, or compulsive dieting/exercising. You will have the victory in Christ Jesus! Expect a miracle in your eating behavior! All things are possible to him who believes! The truth of God's Word will set you free from bondage! Infinite power to walk in your freedom forever! Now is your time for victory! God's fullness of life is yours!

— —

Please send me information about the seminars and newsletter!

Name _____

Address _____

City State Zip _____

Telephone _____

Mail to: Craig S. Hill, **SPIRIT LIFE,** 7955 E. Arapahoe Court, Suite 3100, Englewood, Colorado 80112 (303) 773-2972.

More Faith-Building Books
From
Huntington House

America Betrayed! by Marlin Maddoux. This hard-hitting book exposes the forces in our country which seek to destroy the family, the schools and our values. This book details exactly how the news media manipulates your mind. Marlin Maddoux is the host of the popular, national radio talk show "Point of View."

A Reasonable Reason to Wait by Jacob Aranza, is a frank, definitive discussion on premarital sex — from the biblical viewpoint. God speaks specifically about premarital sex, according to the author. The Bible also provides a healing message for those who have already been sexually involved before marriage. This book is a must reading for every young person — and also for parents — who really want to know the biblical truth on this important subject.

Backward Masking Unmasked by Jacob Aranza. Rock'n'Roll music affects tens of millions of young people and adults in America and around the world. This music is laced with lyrics exalting drugs, the occult, immorality, homosexuality, violence and rebellion. But there is a more sinister danger in this music, according to the author. It's called "backward masking." Teenagers by the millions — who spend hours each day listening to rock music — aren't even aware the messages are there.

Backward Masking Unmasked (cassette tape) by Jacob Aranza. Hear actual satanic messages and judge for yourself.

Computers and the Beast of Revelation by Dr. David Webber and Noah Hutchings. The authors masterfully explain the arrival of this great age of information, particularly relating to computers, in light of Bible prophecy. They share information about computer networks, computer spies and the ultimate computer. Today there are signs all around us that computers are merging all economic transactions into a single, all-knowledgeable system and all nations into one economic system. For centuries scholars have wondered how Revelation 13 might be fulfilled: How could any image or machine command the world to work or buy and sell with code marks and numbers? This book answers that question.

Devil Take the Youngest by Winkie Pratney. This book reveals the war on children being waged in America and the world today. Pratney, a world-renowned author, teacher and conference speaker, relates distinct parallels of the ancient worship of Moloch, where children were sacrificed, to today's tragic abuse, killing and kidnapping of children.

The Divine Connection by Dr. Donald Whitaker. This is a Christian guide of life extension. It specifies biblical principles on how to feel better and live longer and shows you how to experience Divine health, a happier life, relief from stress, a better appearance, a healthier outlook on life, a zest for living and a sound emotional life.

Globalism: America's Demise by William Bowen, Jr. The Globalists — some of the most powerful people on earth — have plans to eliminate God, the family, and the United States as we know it today. Globalism is the vehicle the humanists are using to implement their secular humanistic philosophy to bring about their one-world government. The four goals of Globalism are: 1) a one-world government; 2) a new world religion; 3) a new economic system; 4) a new race of people for the new world order. This book alerts Christians to what Globalists have planned for them.

God's Timetable for the 1980's by Dr. David Webber. This book presents the end-time scenario as revealed in God's Word. It deals with a wide spectrum of subjects including the dangers of the New Age Movement, end-time weather changes, outer space, robots and biocomputers in prophecy. According to the author, the number 666 is occurring more and more frequently in world communications, banking and business. This number will one day polarize the computer code marks and identification numbering systems of the Antichrist, he says.

The Great Falling Away Today by Milton Green. This renowned speaker, whose message changed the life and ministry of evangelist James Robison, shows the joy and peace that comes through deliverance, and cites what the Bible says about today's "great apostasy" and the future of an unrepentant church.

Hearts on Fire by Jimmy Phillips. What is God doing throughout the world? Where is revival taking place? What is the heart's cry of the people? Phillips answers these and other important questions in this delightful book. During his travels as a missionary-evangelist, he has ministered both in the rag cities of India and the largest church in the world, which is in Korea. As you read his story, your heart will be set on fire as you look at the world through his eyes.

The Hidden Dangers of the Rainbow by Constance Cumbey. This national #1 bestseller is a vivid exposé of the New Age Movement which the author reveals as is dedicated to wiping out Christianity and establishing a one-world order. This movement, a vast network of occult organizations, meets the test of prophecy concerning the Antichrist. How are satanists preparing the way for their world leader? Read this carefully documented work and be shocked.

The Hidden Dangers of the Rainbow Tape by Constance Cumbey. Mrs. Cumbey, a trial lawyer from Detroit, Michigan, gives inside information on the New Age Movement in this teaching tape.

Honor Thy Father?? by Meridel Rawlings. Pain and heartache are not the only results when a pastor's family is hit by the agony and humiliation of incest. Out of the ashes of a devastated family comes healing, forgiveness and a timely lesson for all Christians seeking answers amid today's epidemic child abuse, "kiddie porn," flaunted sexual liberality and decaying moral taboos.

How to Cope When You Can't by Don Gossett is a guide to dealing with the everyday stresses and pressures of life. Gossett, a well-known Christian author and evangelist, draws from many personal experiences in this book which brings hope and encouragement for victory in our Lord. The author deals with such contemporary subjects as coping with guilt, raising children, financial difficulties, poverty, a sectarian spirit, the devil's devices, pride, fear and inadequacy, sickness, sorrow and other real problems. This book is a must for Christians who want to be victorious — even when Satan attempts to set them up for defeat and dispair.

How to Grow Up Spiritually by Steve Shamblin. Are you a baby Christian? Are you anxious to be a mature leader? Are you weary of not being spiritually "experienced" enough to counsel others, to take authority over Satan or to evangelize the world? Here's a manual that will get you started — and to help you set your priorities.

More Rock, Country & Backward Masking Unmasked by Jacob Aranza. Aranza's first book, *Backward Masking Unmasked* was a national bestseller. It clearly exposed the backward satanic messages included in a lot of rock and roll music. Now, in the sequel, Aranza gives new information on backward messages. Also, for the first time in Christian literature, he takes a hard look at the content, meaning and dangers of country music. "Rock, though filled with satanism, sex and drugs ... has a hard time keeping up with the cheatin', drinkin' and one-night stands that continue to dominate country music," the author says.

Murdered Heiress ... Living Witness by Dr. Petti Wagner. The victim of a sinister kidnapping and murder plot, the Lord miraculously gave her life back to her. Dr. Wagner — heiress to a large fortune — was kidnapped, tortured, beaten, electrocuted and died. A doctor signed her death certificate, yet she lives today!

Natalie — The Miracle Child by Barry and Cathy Beaver. The heartwarming, inspirational story of miracle child Natalie Beaver. When she was born, her internal organs were outside her body. The doctors said she would never survive. Yet, God performed a miracle and Natalie is healed today.

Rest From the Quest by Elissa Lindsey McClain. This is the candid account of a former New Ager who spent the first 29 years of her life in the New Age Movement, the occult and Eastern mysticism. This is an incredible inside look at what really goes on in the New Age Movement.

The Twisted Cross by Joseph Carr. One of the most important works of our decade, *The Twisted Cross* clearly documents the occult and demonic influence on Adolf Hitler and the Third Reich which led to the killing of more than 6 million Jews. The author even gives specifics of the bizarre way in which Hitler actually became demon-possessed.

Who Will Rise Up? by Jed Smock. This is the incredible — and sometimes hilarious — story of Jed Smock, who with his wife, Cindy, has preached the uncompromising gospel in the malls and on the lawns of hundreds of university campuses throughout this land. They have been mocked, rocked, stoned, mobbed, beaten, jailed, cursed and ridiculed by the students. Yet this former university professor and his wife have seen the miracle-working power of God transform thousands of lives on university campuses.

Yes, send me the following books:

copy / copies of		
America Betrayed! @ $5.95	$
A Reasonable Reason To Wait @ $4.95	$
Backward Masking Unmasked @ $5.95	$
Backward Masking Unmasked Cassette Tape @ $6.95	$
Beast @ $6.95	$
Computers and the Beast of Revelation @ $6.95	$
Devil Take the Youngest @ $6.95	$
Edmund Burke and The Natural Law @ $7.95	$
Globalism: America's Demise @ $6.95	$
God's Timetable for the 1980's @ $5.95	$
Hearts on Fire @ $5.95	$
Honor Thy Father? @ $6.95	$
How to Cope When You Can't @ $6.95	$
How to Grow Up Spiritually @ $6.95	$
More Rock, Country & Backward Masking Unmasked @ $5.95	$
More Rock, Country & Backward Masking Unmasked Tape @ $6.95	$
Murdered Heiress ... Living Witness @ $6.95	$
Natalie @ $4.95	$
Need a Miracle? @ $5.95	$
Rest From the Quest @ $5.95	$
Take Him to the Streets @ $6.95	$
The Agony of Deception @ $6.95	$
The Divine Connection @ $4.95	$
The Great Falling Away Today @ $6.95	$
The Hidden Dangers of the Rainbow @ $6.95	$
The Hidden Dangers of the Rainbow Seminar Tapes @ $19.95	$
The Miracle of Touching @ $5.95	$
The Twisted Cross @ $7.95	$
Where Were You When I Was Hurting? @ $6.95	$
Who Will Rise Up? @ $5.95	$

AT BOOKSTORES EVERYWHERE or order directly from Huntington House, Inc., P.O. Box 53788, Lafayette, LA 70505

Send check/money order or for faster service VISA/Mastercard orders call toll-free 1-800-572-8213. Add: Freight and handling, $1.00 for the first book ordered, 50¢ for each additional book.

Enclosed is $ _____ including postage.

Name _____

Address _____

City _____ State and ZIP _____